## What people are saying about *Personalized Philanthropy...*

*Accompany Steve on his journey in pursuit of the donor-focused fundraising we all claim to espouse. Enlightened fundraisers can use his book as a guide to crossing over from traditional gift planner to courageous champion, starting with one donor and one gift.*

**Alexandra P. Brovey, JD, LLM**
**Senior Director, Gift Planning, North Shore-Long Island Jewish Health System Foundation**
**Past President, Philanthropic Planning Group of Greater New York**

*A unique, personal, smart approach to the charitable giving process—a refreshing look at how to make the right decisions, have the right conversations to result in the right gifts. I know that my students will be encouraged (maybe even required) to read this book.*

**Davida Isaacson**
**Fundraising Consultant, Educator**

*This book contains what's missing in CFRE education on "planned giving." Thought-provoking, creative, practical examples that enable you to put the ideas into action. These gift design principles will help gift officers step out of their silos and into twenty-first-century fundraising for major impact.*

**Eden Graber, CFRE**
**Independent Consultant in Fundraising and Marketing Communications**
**Former Director of Development, New York, American Committee for Weizmann Institute of Science**

*Steve Meyers encourages us to bring down the institutional silos that limit the real potential of donors and institutions. He illustrates specific donor-focused techniques that have educated and inspired more meaningful and rewarding blended gifts. His "apps" should be in all our tool kits!*

**Andrea Hill**
**Senior Director of Individual and Major Gifts, Food Bank For New York City**

*Steve's book provides a dramatic, holistic, inspiring donor-centric approach to fundraising to guide both donors and development professionals on how to make miracles happen.*

**Lisa Lager**
**Philanthropic Advisor**
**Board Member, Philanthropic Planning Group of Greater New York**

*All who engage in encouraging and inspiring charitable giving have a great new resource in Personalized Philanthropy—both seasoned professionals and those just beginning their careers in fundraising. Steve and I think alike. I like what he has written, and I think you will too.*

**David Dunlop**
**Senior Development Officer (1959–95), Cornell University**

*Steven Meyers'* **Personalized Philanthropy** *demonstrates gift-planning vehicles that cross the artificial lines of annual, major, and planned gifts. This original approach benefits charitable organizations and helps advisors such as gift planners, attorneys, certified public accountants, and financial planners put donors first. I highly recommend it.*

**William A. Snyder, Esq.**
**Attorney and Adjunct Professor of Law, University of Miami Law School**
**Graduate Program in Estate Planning**

*A* must *for beginners to advanced professionals. Fresh perspective helps boards and bosses give successful programs their due and influence to tear down silos. In fact, "Counting, Numbers, Value and the Big Picture" is worth the price of the book just for this chapter alone!*

**Margaret M. Holman**
**President, Holman Consulting**
**Author and Adjunct Professor, NYU**
**President Emerita, Philanthropic Planning Group of Greater New York**

*What possible benefits would* **Personalized Philanthropy** *have for me, an estate planning lawyer for over fifty years? Many! This book is not just for fundraisers, but for lawyers, financial planners, and other advisors seeking innovative approaches to serving client needs in clear and dramatic ways.*

**Peter J. Strauss**
**Distinguished Adjunct Professor of Law, New York Law School**
**Fellow, American College of Trust and Estate Counsel**
**Fellow, National Academy of Elder Law Attorneys**

*As a wealth manager, and having worked on behalf of charities, I can tell you* **Personalized Philanthropy** *is a breakthrough whose time has come! As competition for private wealth clients increases, these matrix-busting personalized gift applications will make all the difference.*

**Kenneth Bierman**
**Senior Director, Wealth Management, BNY Mellon**

*In* **Personalized Philanthropy**, *Steve gives us the gift of a new way to design philanthropic strategies. He shows us a way to focus on donor goals first and institutional needs second. This should be mandatory reading for every family wealth advisor.*

**Timothy J. Belber, JD, AEP**
**Author, *The Middle Way: Using Balance to Create Successful Family Wealth Transition Plans***

*I like this book. It certainly matches my experience and observations.*
**Jonathan G. Tidd, Esq.**

# Personalized Philanthropy

## Crash the Fundraising Matrix

Steven L. Meyers, PhD

**Personalized Philanthropy: Crash the Fundraising Matrix**

One of the **In the Trenches™** series

Published by
CharityChannel Press, an imprint of CharityChannel LLC
424 Church Street, Suite 2000
Nashville, TN 37219 USA

CharityChannel.com

ISBN Print Book: 978-1-938077-67-8 | ISBN eBook: 978-1-938077-68-5

Library of Congress Control Number: 2015930058

13 12 11 10 9 8 7 6 5 4 3 2 1

Printed in the United States of America

This and most CharityChannel Press books are available at special quantity discounts for bulk purchases for sales promotions, premiums, fundraising, or educational use.  For information, contact CharityChannel Press, 424 Church Street, Suite 2000, Nashville, TN 37219 USA. +1 949-589-5938

## Publisher's Acknowledgments

This book was produced by a team dedicated to excellence; please send your feedback to editors@charitychannel.com.

We first wish to acknowledge the tens of thousands of peers who call CharityChannel.com their online professional home. Your enthusiastic support for the **In the Trenches™** series is the wind in our sails.

Members of the team who produced this book include:

### *Editors*

**Acquisitions Editor:** Linda Lysakowski

**Comprehensive Editor:** Barbara Yeager

**Copy Editor:** Stephen Nill

### *Production*

**In the Trenches Series Design:** Deborah Perdue

**Layout Editor:** Jill McLain

### *Administrative*

**CharityChannel LLC:** Stephen Nill, CEO

**Marketing and Public Relations:** John Millen and Linda Lysakowski

# About the Author

Steven L. Meyers, Ph.D., is Vice President in the Center for Personalized Philanthropy at the American Committee for the Weizmann Institute of Science. Steve is a primary developer of personalized philanthropy, based on the mantra of "the right gift, for the right purpose, for the right donor." His innovative donor-focused gift designs, especially a series of arrangements he calls "killer apps," combine the full spectrum of current and future gifts so that donors can create a lasting legacy with impact and recognition that begins now. Steve joined the American Committee of the Weizmann Institute of Science in 1995 and now serves as Vice President of its Center of Personalized Philanthropy, as well as a member of its management team and total financial resource development strategy group. He holds a Master's Degree in Organization and Management from Antioch University and a Ph.D. from the University of Buffalo. Steven has published in *The Journal of Gift Planning* and is a contributing author for the Planned Giving Design Center, the Elite Advisor Report of CEG International Group, and eJewish Philanthropy. He speaks frequently at national and regional gift planning conferences on donor-focused giving and "Planned Giving in the Big Picture." Steve strongly believes in building a pioneering culture of teamwork and collaboration and most enjoys helping donors realize ways they can help make miracles happen at the Weizmann Institute and other organizations close to their hearts.

# Dedication

This book is dedicated to my Aunt Anna Tender and generations past, who showed me the way; and to the next generations of enlightened generalists to whom we entrust the future of philanthropy.

# Author's Acknowledgments

When I crashed my own Matrix and the silos and blinders came down, I suddenly realized that philanthropy was a much larger field of interest than I had ever imagined and that there was so much more to explore, discover, and create. Personalized philanthropy became a quest to restore creativity and balance to this important work.

I am grateful to friends and colleagues who inspired and persistently encouraged me to crash my own Matrix and then pursue the concepts that ultimately became the core of this book. I am thankful for mind mapping and other ways of capturing creative disorder and embracing uncertainty, and for William Carlos Williams, well, just because he was right: There are no ideas but in things.

Opportunity as well as editorial discipline came from longtime friend, Barbara Yeager. Inspiration from many colleagues, teachers, and advisors including David Dunlop, Bill Samers, and Stacy Sulman, Mark Kalish, Davida Isaacson, Margaret Holman, Vivian Kantrow, Cindy O'Donnell, Robert King, Marshall Levin, Larry Blumberg, Mitch Wein, Phil Cubeta, Doug White, Richard Enslein, Jon Tidd, Eden Graber, and Steven Steinberg. And vision from the many donors who continuously helped open doors to entirely new ways of thinking about philanthropy.

Most especially I thank my wife, Dorothy, and the godfathers and godmothers of this book. I identify them as those who would never have let me forget, were I not to have said "yes" when publisher Stephen Nill serendipitously rode into town on his *deus ex machina*.

Final thanks to those who remind me daily what counts, as in the key to flying: The thing you push against is the thing that lifts you up.

# Contents

# Summary of Chapters

**Counting, Numbers, Value, and the Big Picture.** We all have to address (and quantify) our effectiveness at some point, as well as the donor's. What difference does it make that you are there, and what are you really trying to achieve? We examine ways to measure effectiveness and what *really* constitutes fundraising achievement in an unfiltered and true sense.

**Being the Change and Making your Own Shift.** I outline the three key things in your development culture that need to change if you hope to institutionalize a more personalized approach to gift planning.

# Foreword

**D**onor-focused philanthropy has become a cliché. After decades of "it's all-about-our-organization fundraising," charities thought it wise to take into account what *donors* might need from the gift transaction. For a long time, this meant little more than applying planned giving techniques, many of which provide payments or an income to the donor in exchange for giving up an asset. But those methods, taken from the shelf of the 1969 Tax Act and which, by the way, can be immensely beneficial to both the donor and the charity, are still much more transactional than emotionally comprehensive. More recently, and a bit more expansively, the question has grown to include what donors need, not only from a financial perspective, but from a mission perspective—the donor's mission, not just the charity's.

But while that's the better idea, until now it's been pretty much only an idea. The words *donor-focused philanthropy* sound nice, but there hasn't been much to concretely define them or put them to some strategic use.

Steven Meyers has finally broken through the linguistic and strategic logjam to make sense of connecting donor and charities in a way that will, and already does at some organizations, change the way money is raised. It's not just a new twist to take into account a roller-coaster economy and it's not just a new gimmick to address what has come to be known as the great generational wealth transfer. Using a metaphor of an imprisoning Matrix—the typical development office with its goals and deadlines—Steve artfully and persuasively works through and explains three concepts: virtual endowments, philanthropic equity gifts, and step-up gifts. Each captures what's wrong with the current fundraising model and provides a basis for improving it.

This is not to say that fundraisers today are doing a poor job. Quite the contrary: those who work at charities are doing yeoman's work to make their organizations better as they pursue their missions. But it is also true that development offices can be bureaucratic and, because of inherent limitations, much more could be done. In fact, as donor-focused philanthropy has been a personal cause of mine for many years, I have seen how many organizations limit their ability to raise funds simply because they are not fully engaged with the donor's needs or desires. But to be engaged, fundraisers need to ask a whole different set of questions. Steve guides us through those questions and helps us make meaning of the responses we are likely to get from donors. Doing that, of course, will enhance donors' appreciation for the work charities do and, yes, increase their support.

This, Steve calls personalized philanthropy. As he says, "I want to know why all philanthropy is not already personalized philanthropy." I do too.

**Doug White**

Author, *Abusing Donor Intent: The Robertson Family's Epic Lawsuit Against Princeton University*

Director, Master of Science Program in Fundraising Management, Columbia University

# Publisher's Note

As the publisher, my normal and preferred place is behind the scenes, supporting the author in the challenging but rewarding journey of creating, polishing, and publishing a book. Steven Meyers, though, asked me to break the mold (or should I say "crash the Matrix"?) of how we do things by sharing my thoughts about this book with you, the reader.

This is no ordinary book, and it's not just the fact that it's our first full-color, hardback edition, enabling us to showcase the illustrations created by the author himself. What makes it extraordinary is what it represents: a movement in the field of philanthropy.

When Steven and I first talked about his vision for this book, I instantly grasped its importance. As it happens, before moving into publishing, I spent three-plus decades practicing law and consulting, with a significant part of those years devoted to gift planning and fund development program management. In the early nineties, I was Senior VP of Development at a large nonprofit hospital chain, with only the chain's CEO and COO above me. Taking advantage of my rank, I quickly rebuilt the fund development program from the ground up, focusing on six- and seven-figure gifts from private donors. We were structuring gifts in creative ways that made a great deal of sense to the donors and, from a long-term viewpoint, the organization. (Oh, how I wish I'd had a time machine so that I could have transported to the future to learn about Steven's "killer apps," which he discusses in these pages!)

By my lights, within two years our admittedly unorthodox approach was succeeding. We had attracted a number of donors who were creating large structured gifts, making major pledges, and so on. Most importantly, we were building a kind of momentum that I was sure would continue into the years ahead.

Yet I found it exceedingly hard to quantify our success and justify the program to the board. Sure, there were real numbers that showed *some* of what was going on, but I was constantly explaining why the bigger picture just wasn't being represented in the financial statements. The groundwork that was laid had value far into the future, but I struggled to show it. It was as if we were planting a vast apple orchard but could show the value only by the first few apples that were appearing.

One way or another, this scenario plays out at countless organizations, year after year. Even worse, gift officers do not always have the kind of rank inside their organizations that I enjoyed in the setting I just described. Show me a gift officer at *any* rank, and I'll show you someone who is probably trapped, knowingly or not, in the Matrix—a prisoner to the silos that so many organizations erect.

*Personalized Philanthropy: Crash the Fundraising Matrix* shows us how to crash the Matrix and finally become empowered to truly focus on the donor's philanthropic dreams while advancing the organization farther than ever imagined.

Given what's at stake, if you, gentle reader, are waiting for permission to crash *your* organization's Matrix, don't. If some in your organization don't get it, hand them this book and help them break free too.

**Stephen Nill, JD, GPC**
Publisher

# Introduction

In the post-planned giving era, fundraising frameworks are in flux.

Planned giving was "the next big thing" in the 1990s, but no more. Now it's come of age. Back then, many fundraisers were entering this field. Today, the economics have prompted increasing numbers of development departments to merge planned, annual, and major giving. Is there really a shift going on? If so, what does it mean for your practice? How will fundraising be done in the future?

A sure sign of this shift is all the talk about donor-focused giving in recent years. It's the new by-word. Sensitivity to donors' interests has always been key and now there are some very good theorists writing and speaking on this subject. I've noticed, though, that *all* these experts seem to operate in the theater of annual giving, major giving, or planned giving. *Very few* practitioners focus on the *design of integrated, full-spectrum, donor-focused gifts. None* treats this as the core of an entire discipline of gift planning in itself. I do.

There seems to be a "story gap"—scant sources that demonstrate any specific techniques for designing blended planned and outright gifts in a truly donor-focused, holistic way. The syllabus is all "annual, major, and planned." The syllabus on frameworks of philanthropy has yet to be written that includes integrated, full-spectrum, donor-focused gift strategies. I am aware of only a *single* classroom where this type of fundraising is being taught, though there may be many that talk about it. There are few presentations, articles, or books on the process of donor-focused giving and fundraising, or on its impact on the organization. *Yet, at the same time that the conversation about the centrality of donors is evolving and heating up, the iceberg that is the development office and all its structures and subdivisions seems to be melting.*

My goal is to overcome enough inertia and baggage from the past to promote some real change; to provide you with reproducible gift design models for this new era—starting points—for your own work with donors; to encourage personalized philanthropy and gift design to evolve in classrooms; and to help *you*, even as one individual, to restore creativity to your practice of charitable gift planning, whether you are a gift officer in a development office or a philanthropist in your own living room

Today, I call them virtual endowments, philanthropic equity gifts, and step-up gifts—the three game-changing "killer apps" (applications) described in this book. In prior years, I have given them various names as my focus has sharpened and perspective changed. An important truth is that my understanding came about and was crystallized, so to speak, through fieldwork in the trenches with actual donors. Like any new technology, once employed and understood, these applications of personalized philanthropy seem to acquire a power of their own as game-changers.

In the development office, implementing these personalized gift designs promotes synapse-like new pathways that build collaboration and integration across organizational sectors and department boundaries. With our most ardent donors, they start conversations that end in very satisfying gifts that might never have seen the light of day. Yet at the organizational level, they represent a change in the normal order of things by disrupting the traditional boundary lines between annual, major, and planned gift fundraising departments.

I've built this book around understanding four essential features necessary for a multidimensional, holistic, and donor-focused philanthropy system. They are:

◆ Designing and shaping gifts to mesh compelling interests with compelling need.

◆ Radically rethinking endowment and the grail of fundraising.

◆ Donor engagements utilizing a personalized gift design process to move beyond conventional solicitations.

◆ Counting and reporting gifts in a multidimensional, donor-focused way.

Sometimes I am asked why I am giving away "proprietary" knowledge about multidimensional gift design. My first thought was, *it's just not much fun to work in a vacuum.* In reality, I can give this technology away, but you cannot really benefit from it without addressing the cultural issues of your organization—and some of those issues are written into policy. Of course, it's easier and more productive for everyone involved to conduct personalized philanthropy if you have enlightened policies in place for counting all types of gifts and have already lowered the boundaries between departments. But even then, I want to make a declarative statement: it's not an absolute prerequisite to work in a utopian environment. Nobody does! Even if you're working in an organization where deferred or revocable gifts don't count—or count for an amount well below their true impact. Don't fall into the trap of thinking you are powerless to act. You can begin to experiment with gifts that cross the typical boundaries between major and planned silos. Just one donor's excitement about this new way to give-with-impact-now can spark the change and be the catalyst for organization-wide awakening.

Throughout your reading you'll have to keep in mind that it is somewhat inevitable that this book is as much bio as it is info. I hope you will enjoy this book and use it to crash through your own fundraising Matrix. It's not so difficult. You begin with yourself.

# Chapter One

## Two Cultures of Fundraising: Preparing to Crash Your Fundraising Matrix

### IN THIS CHAPTER

---→ Across the great divide: which side are you on?

---→ If my Matrix crashes, will I fall forever, without end? What comes after that?

---→ How do you begin to rethink the balance between donor- and institution-focus?

---→ Hints for diagnosing and negotiating fundraising silos and boundaries

You can tell easily whether you're working in an institutionally focused culture or a donor-focused culture. It's by the script. For me, the conversation often starts with, "Hi Steve. Do you have a minute?"

In the early days, when this call came, I was content in my "planned giving" silo and the major gift officer on the other end of the line was happy in hers—and never the twain shall meet. She was calling me from her car on the way to see her prospect and wanted to pitch a charitable gift annuity to an 89 year-old donor, so she needed the rate and the charitable deduction for a person of the donor's age. No problem for me to pull up my calculator and give her the info. I didn't really mind, with the proviso that I could prepare a full illustration and gift disclosure before the gift would be completed. Gift closes: planned and major gift officers both happy; donor happy; our boss happy. We each go our separate ways. We were completely oblivious to the other possibilities of what might have been, nor did we much care.

Twenty years later, the conversation is different.

"Hi Steve. Do you have some time to talk strategy? I'm going to meet with a donor. We've become close over the years. I want to go over a couple of ideas before I call her. I haven't decided anything yet." She's 89 years old; been a donor for fifteen years and made modest annual gifts for the last ten of them, but the recent one was the largest. Last year, her husband died of Alzheimer's; now her kids are grown and independent on their own. She was a biology major in college, but never got to finish school herself. We have a note in the file that she had us in her will, but it's very old and who knows if it's even real. What do you think we should talk about?"

First, we listen. Then we listen some more. We explore an overall strategy with this donor, who ultimately decides to create a professorial chair, preferably in brain research. But first, she starts off with a simple annual scholarship based on continuing her current pattern of annual gifts for the next eight or nine years; then, she arranges to top off her giving with a bequest of the larger part of her estate in order to expand her endowment fund from supporting a scholarship to a chair. Oh, and along the way, this year she decides to sweeten things and establish a charitable gift annuity. The annuity, though modest by some standards, represents the largest transfer she's done for our charity yet. Her plan for the scholarship growing into the chair is recognized and starts immediately—and a highly *personalized philanthropic plan* is in place that can be counted in our campaign for this year. Agreement is written, gift closes: planned and major gift officers both happy; donor happy; boss happy. Gift design team celebrates a win and looks forward to working together again.

Both of these conversations are happening today and it's been that way for years. We are two cultures, teetering back and forth between two realities. The traditional and dominant culture is a one-dimensional, hierarchical, and highly structured set of departments promoting and valuing different kinds of giving (annual, capital, endowment, planned) based on immediate financial value and utility, with the institution's current fundraising needs and goals at the center.

The other, nontraditional, personalized philanthropy culture tends toward a more collaborative, curiosity-driven culture, where there are few(er) boundaries and a sense that anything might happen, with a fully transparent counting system that reflects the donor at the center and takes the long-term view.

The sheer *abundance* of approaches for translating a donor's passion into gifts that are rewarding for the donor and for the organization cannot be matched in a conventionally organized fundraising department, where scarcity rules. The separation and competition of annual, major, and planned gifts in conventional departments simply does not allow an integrated gift design that blends current and future gifts in a unified plan. So many fundraising organizations are blind to this that it makes you want to ask: what is really going on here? Can you relate to these experiences in your own personal gift practice and in your organization? If so, you might agree with me that it's almost as if we live in the anti-utopian world of the movie, *The Matrix*. Remember?

## The Fundraising Matrix—System Failure

Andy and Larry Wachowski's 1999 film, *The Matrix*, and its two sequels, depicted a dystopia in which Earth is dominated by sentient machines. The machines rebelled against humanity, growing people in pods solely to extract their energy, while keeping their minds under control by cybernetic implants connecting them to a simulated reality called the Matrix.

The simulation was indistinguishable from "true" reality and most humans connected to the Matrix were unaware of its true nature. The central characters in the three Matrix films were able to gain superhuman abilities within the Matrix by using their understanding of its true nature to manipulate its physical laws.

It often appears that we operate in a fundraising Matrix—a synthetic, artificial environment in which the development office grapples with a need to feed the campaign of the moment, rather than the desires, needs, and true interests of our donors. This is contrasted to the more organic holistic world of donor-focused giving.

The fundraising Matrix drains energy from fundraisers and donors:

◆ Institutional advancement culture takes precedence over, yet depends upon, lasting donor engagement.

◆ Narrow fundraising goals and organizational structures (annual/major/planned) obscure the real capacity of donors to support organizations close to their hearts.

◆ Gift officers who could potentially offer leadership to their organizations remain locked in the "box"—their narrow silos— of planned or major giving. Often, sadly, it is because jobs have been eliminated or because of staff reorganizations that integrate planned and major gifts. Sometimes, even more sadly, it is by their own choice. Some prefer a silo like an iceberg that is melting to none at all.

As Morpheus says to Neo in the first episode,

*The Matrix is everywhere. It is all around us....*

*Unfortunately, no one can be told what the Matrix is.*

*You have to see it for yourself.*

Both organizations and their most ardent supporters ultimately lose from the failure to have gift strategies that strike a balance between the donor's interests and the institution's goals. In the fundraising profession, the Matrix limits our potential to develop new best practices and constrains the careers of gift officers, who cannot evolve into the best fundraising professionals they could be.

The fundraising Matrix is the fragmented world that gift officers and donors must face. There are no alternative universes: essentially, two worlds that seem in mighty conflict, because while one is institution-focused, the other

### Across the Great Divide:
### The Moat between Planned and Major Gifts

The two cultures exist and coexist in almost every organization, whether it is large or small. For some reason, the smaller shops seem to model themselves along the same lines as the larger ones; meaning that even if there are only one or two fundraisers, they (somehow) will manage to find a silo or a channel and build a moat between them, carving out separate territories for annual, capital, endowment, or planned giving. Why? Why? Is it really only about the "credit?" Where is the *donor* in this picture?

Perhaps the challenges smaller shops face now—raising more funds with ever fewer resources and fundraisers—make it essential for them to function more as generalists and find ways to integrate planned and major giving into a full gift planning perspective and, perhaps ultimately, a donor-focused approach. What I've found from observing as well as reflecting on my own experience is that a book about becoming a donor-focused culture is just as relevant, or more so, to a smaller organization as to a larger one.

**observation**

is donor-focused. We drift back and forth between these two cultures. Most of the time, we do not even realize when we slip between the two worlds; other times, we are shocked by extreme turbulence at the margins. However, while the institution-focused culture dominates, I believe the donor-focused culture always has had a place; it has been there like a wave running through fundraising, or a tide rising from time to time, and then receding.

*I believe that the aim and purpose of all fundraising is deceptively simple: to mesh the compelling interests of the donor to the compelling needs of your organization.* But not every gift officer or organization holds this worldview. It sounds like a very neat equation. Donor on one side, institution on the other, perfectly balanced. Personalized philanthropy and conventional philanthropy are markedly different. As illustrated so well by the words "institutional advancement," gift officers have a vested interest in putting a thumb on one side of the scale. In that case, the donor's and the institution's interests and needs are often seen as competing rather than compelling, driving them apart rather than together.

Let's imagine that there are two model scripts for talking with donors: one conventional, based on institution-focused fundraising, and the other based on donor-focused personalized philanthropy.

Under a conventional, institution-focused "solicitation" model, you will follow a script familiar to most fundraisers. It is relatively straightforward, with clear boundaries, rules of protocol and conventions: it will be the "ask." The gift officer has something specific in mind to ask for, perhaps cash to be used for a new program, capital building, or other project. The institution has identified this as a priority worthy of the donor's funding. The gift officer's responsibility, sometimes with a lay partner or executive officer of the institution, is to explain the need and conduct the ask. If you are the fundraiser or the executive, you are well-stocked with facts, figures, and even photos of the donor's name on a building.

According to the script, after the "niceties" and other small talk (for a specific number of minutes), the fundraisers make a presentation. It is clear they will be asking for a specific amount of money, generally cash, to be paid within a certain time.

"Would you consider a gift of $_____ for _____?" Pause for thunderous silence. Woe unto the fundraiser who breaks that silence before the donor.

A conventional solicitation can truly be a charged moment, both for donor and fundraiser. I heard a wonderful presentation not long ago that compared this moment and the *dramatis personae* to those of Shakespeare's *King Lear*. It may sound far-fetched, but those of us who have actually participated in that scene know that it is a moment of intensely heightened awareness and high anxiety. Time stands still. (If only the King had had a lead trust!)

Many fundraisers, and there are times I've counted myself among them, are uncomfortable with the artificial relationship created in these solicitations. You can really feel burdened by having to carry off a synthetic or inauthentic asking style, which somehow seems to be expected in these circumstances. In a case like this, it is a good idea to ask for help. Organizations often identify some staff as closers and bring them in like designated hitters from outside, because they are at some distance emotionally and personally from the donor-target. A lot of times, that's me: the hired gun. I do closing well.

I will never forget when I was asked to join a colleague with a solicitation of a donor who, after that required (and scripted) silence, said "yes" to our solicitation for a million-dollar pledge from her estate. I will swear that the face of my colleague turned red and heat waves actually came out of the top of her head! Everything is focused on that one moment. High anxiety.

## Full-spectrum Philanthropy

Personalized philanthropy, on the other hand, is not just an ask. In full-spectrum personalized philanthropy, the ask becomes a conversation, utilizing all the possible building blocks to mesh donors' and institutions' needs. The approach is so organic and relationship-based that a gift just seems to grow from its own soil. Compared with institution-focused conventional "asks," solicitations in personalized philanthropy might appear chaotic, disorderly, and accidental, like any authentic conversation would. Authentic. The greatest secret of planned giving, at least that practiced by David Dunlop and a few others, is that you never have to ask. Given the advances made possible through the gift designs of personalized philanthropy, I would agree with Louis Pasteur, who famously said, "Chance favors the prepared mind." If you're doing it right, the gifts will tend to come to you. Yes, but I also tend to push the river, more than just a little bit. I know gift officers who understand this in their gut. If you are lucky, they will confide the truth to you—that they experience such conversations as exhilarating high-flying and breath-taking, yet with rewards far greater than any they might have calculated in advance.

## Are You in the Matrix?

In the film, most humans could not tell that they were living in an artificial system. In a similar vein, even if everything seems to be going well in your own fundraising silo, you might not realize you are *feeding* an organizational goal at the expense of your donors' true commitment and capacity.

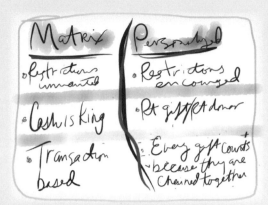

If these conditions seem familiar, then it's time to crash your Matrix:

◆ *"You didn't raise that!"* Fundraisers who preceded you raised a lot of bequest expectancies and other deferred gifts, but they were never given credit, since those gifts had no immediate financial impact on campaign goals. They left. Now those gifts are coming in big time! The irony is, you are not given credit either, because *you* didn't raise those dollars.

◆ *"Stop in the name of love."* You're working hard on a campaign that has room for only certain types of gifts, so naturally it excludes many potential supporters. You have to hesitate to project any openness to acquire deferred or revocable gifts—even from your most loyal and ardent donors—because they will be hurt. Their gifts won't be counted toward that goal, even when those are the best gifts they can make. To promote the right gift would be disappointing for your donors and career suicide for you.

◆ *"Deja vu all over again."* You find yourself proposing the same gift vehicle with few variations to every donor, usually cash now or a short-term pledge. What's the point of doing discovery or even listening? You really are in a box, aren't you?

◆ *"It's the same old song."* It has become your job to convince donors that unrestricted gifts are the most valuable for the organization, yet they've got to pass or do so much less—and it's so ironic—*because* they feel passionately about your mission and want something with programmatic impact now.

Much of our time with donors under this new personalized full-spectrum paradigm is spent discovering and understanding the compelling interests that are the natural drivers of donors' charitable impulse and philanthropy.

## Personalized Philanthropy, the Matrix, and Social Capital

Personalized philanthropy challenges the Matrix. Fundraising solicitations no longer have to be focused primarily on meeting the goals of the siloed annual, major gift or planned gift campaigns. Instead, the goal shifts to *achieving something of moment both for the donor and the organization.*

The lens of personalized philanthropy enables us to look at each gift for each donor as the balancing point of a scale or equation. On the *donor side* is *compelling interest* and desire to for impact, recognition, and legacy. On the *institution side* are enduring and compelling needs of institutions we care about. If they are clearly articulated, donors will resonate with one or another or all of them in a very personal way.

*Between the two sides* are all the tools of philanthropy: current and future gifts, gifts that provide life income, gifts with benefits that skip generations, etc., etc. This also includes all the arrangements that can be brought to the table by estate and financial professionals. Their vehicles can be crucial to the success of a plan. In personalized philanthropy, they are still important, not solely as products to "sell," but instead they are the philanthropic building blocks with which gift officers and professional advisors may create something new and important for the donor and the institution. This effort can be fulfilling for advisors, who work to create social capital for their clients, as well as for charities, whose work is to translate that wealth into social impact.

## Crashing *Your* Fundraising Matrix—Going from Zero to One

Gift planners operating in the silo of the annual campaign may be perfectly content with their skill set to raise annual gifts, and yet be completely blind to the possibility of major philanthropic opportunity lurking among the annual donors. Once you wake up and realize that you are operating in an artificially created and synthetic environment—The Fundraising Matrix— you begin to have the means to escape the trap: focus on the donor. When donor-focus is accepted as the organizational norm, fundraisers can operate seemingly outside the laws of physics—the channels of conventional transactional fundraising, crossing boundaries (almost) at will, yet with the blessings of their fully engaged stakeholders.

That's the ideal world outside the Matrix. But, what if it's not the goal in *your* shop? What if the Matrix is strong in your shop? The goal in your development office is *complete separation* between annual giving and bequest giving. Perhaps someone in leadership mistakenly believes that bequest donors will feel relieved of the responsibility (or their joy) to continue or increase current gifts. If that were true, you really should have separate staff "owning" their donors; you'll want to make sure the donors designated for each do not interact; and you'll insist on having separate goals and organizational structures for each division in your development office. Ironically, most of the personalized philanthropy apps I'll describe in a later chapter actually encourage deferred donors to enhance their current giving.

For too many of my friends and colleagues, the powerful Matrix scenario is not imaginary but real. The silos are strong and high. Staff in the planned giving department can't access the frequent annual givers, even though *we* know they are the best likely prospects for bequests. It is really not uncommon to see this kind of division even in organizations that receive 30 percent of their *total* gift revenues from bequests!

You might ask: *What would happen if the boundaries suddenly came down?* Many organizations get this opportunity to breach silos or change reporting relationships when staff turns over. Unfortunately, the stories we hear are often of bad outcomes.

The worst-case scenarios are when (1) management decides not to fill the slot when the planned giving specialist leaves, and the organization simply walks away from bequests and planned gifts because they seem to have stopped producing. Or, (2) the administration simply integrates all the planned and major giving staff, bringing them together without thought into one department.

Fundraisers trapped in the silo of annual, major, or planned gifts still have some solid domain skills. Much could be gained if they are able to take their old domain knowledge into a new area, and have it be considered an asset in the new domain. But if there is no big-picture view and the skill's not valued, your organization would be at risk for one of those worst-case scenarios.

On the other hand, even in highly siloed development offices, I think success can still be found if you look for those places, often at the very edges of the system, where the boundaries are more likely to be permeable. You just need to reach out for one friend or colleague across the aisle who would like to reach back to you. Then ask for clearance to create a pilot

## The Original Flexible Endowment

One of the true pioneers of personalized philanthropy is David Dunlop. David is widely credited with first developing the "CPI" gifts, with annual payments indexed to the consumer price index. Credit is certainly due.

These original "flexible endowments" are the cornerstone of the technology that enables personalized philanthropy today. They created the possibility for unifying the distinct worlds of annual, major, and planned gift transactions and enabling their transformation into a holistic donor-focused enterprise.

In David's groundbreaking and original work, there is a clear parallel to breakthroughs in basic science research, where a discovery is made but the full impact is not felt until many years in the future. So it was with the electron, originally celebrated as useless upon its discovery one-hundred years ago because nobody thought they needed it, and upon which today rests the entire underpinning of our technology and online culture. So too today, from the concept of flexible endowments, is emerging a new discipline of personalized gift design.

project, or call it an experiment. Or, if asking permission first is bound to be met with, "no," forge ahead and ask for forgiveness afterward.

Find a way to add value on a case-by-case basis. You don't have to change everything to make the world (or just your world) a better place—you just have to go from zero to one.

## Why Isn't All Philanthropy Personalized Philanthropy?

Not long ago, I had the privilege of meeting Berta Strulovici, the founding director of the Israel National Center for Personalized Medicine, Weizmann Institute's multidisciplinary collaboration for bringing the best minds together to advance personalized science from the bench to the bedside. After her presentation, I asked her about the latest developments at her center. I mentioned the new name of our department, which was formerly known as Planned Giving and is now the Center for Personalized

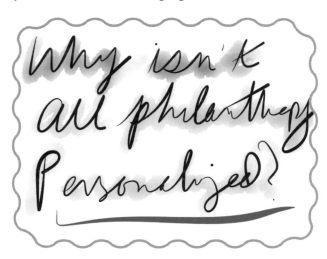

philanthropy. I asked her, "Why isn't all medicine personalized?" She told me that before long, it will be. Then she asked me, "Why isn't all philanthropy personalized philanthropy?" I answered, "Hopefully, before long, all philanthropy will be personalized, too."

In personalized medicine, scientific progress in genetics, proteomics, and rapid screening for drug design point to a future when medical treatments will be based on our own individual makeup, and drugs will work for each person, in the right dose, the first time. Gone will be the days when every patient was given the same medicine, where it might work for them, or it might not. In fact, this transformation is already under way in many fields.

There are new tools in personalized philanthropy, too, and they are sparking a new kind of partnership between donors and fundraisers.

Donors were formerly expected to make gifts when asked, as a kind of "tax." They had limited choices, were subject to off-the-shelf solicitations—often unrelated to their interests—for "annual," "major," and "planned" gifts. They had very little to say about the impact or use of their funds, because the ideal gift was always considered unrestricted, except for the top of the top-tier gifts for special campaigns.

Personalized philanthropy places all the building blocks in the hands of each donor, and actively encourages donors to restrict their gifts to achieve their greatest impact. The first aim of our fundraising conversation is discovery—the match of a donor's most compelling interests with the organization's most compelling needs. When we achieve this, we know we will be able to build a great gift. Even the most modest of contributions can advance a donor's impact, in the context of the donor's overall philanthropic life.

This concept of the right gift, for the right donor, for the right purpose, is an exact analogy to personalized medicine. With every donor our challenge is to capture this "rightness."

## Nature or Nurture?

I have been fortunate to be associated with the American Committee for the Weizmann Institute of Science for nearly twenty years, first as its national director of planned giving and more recently as vice president of its aptly named Center for Personalized Philanthropy. The organization from which much of my inspiration springs is the Weizmann Institute of Science, Israel's home of basic curiosity-driven research. The Weizmann Institute has been consistently voted in *Science Magazine's* survey as the best place in the world to do science outside the United States. Weizmann's American fundraising organization sees in the institute a wonderful and powerful model of what can be accomplished in an interdisciplinary, collaborative setting, amid total academic freedom where innovation and risk-taking are encouraged for the benefit of all.

This has created a feeling among colleagues that there is a partnership between science and philanthropy. In the same way the Weizmann Institute is a great place to do science, our goal is for the American Committee for Weizmann to be one of the great places in the United States for donors to do their philanthropy.

As we explore this new and evolving model of personalized philanthropy, our own gift officers increasingly have the *opportunity* to move away from a transactional "sales" model, towards that of being "gift navigators." We feel we are helping donors find their way to the right gifts (at the right time and for the right purpose) to achieve maximum impact on the organization and get the current satisfaction they deserve.

Of course, it is important to state that while I have been associated for many years with the American Committee for the Weizmann Institute, in this book I am writing about my own experiences and not speaking for Weizmann or the American Committee. Still, it's also fair to say that we have, in a sense (at least on a good day), crashed the Matrix to create a culture of personalized philanthropy. For that, I'm very grateful.

How do the unique culture and values of *your* organization express themselves in your fundraising culture? Finding that connection can inspire more organic and, probably, more productive conversations with your most committed donors.

## To Recap

◆ The traditional categories of annual, major, and planned gifts mean something to development officers, but they mean nothing to donors and to their advisors. They may actually be obstacles to creating a meaningful gift for a donor with a passion for a particular area of your mission.

◆ Donors' resources come in many forms, and larger gifts with greater impact are possible when current and future income and/or asset streams can be combined. Again, this is not widely considered by gift planners, or, for that matter, financial and estate professionals, who often focus on a transaction rather than the lifetime value of a donor.

◆ How would your fundraising results differ if you treated gift vehicles as building blocks rather than sequential, fragmented asks.

◆ Consider the current fundraising culture in your organization. Where does it rest in the balance between institutional focus and donor focus?

◆ To offer the options of personalized philanthropy to your donors, you *must* have access to committed donors who have already made gifts, whether annual, major or planned. If you work in a strongly siloed development shop, can you create an opportunity to experiment, perhaps by working with one colleague in annual giving and one very passionate, loyal donor?

◆ Try rewriting the scripts you use with donors and colleagues. Ask, "How could we make greater impact, and start it sooner?"

◆ Try to imagine a conversation with a donor in which you explain the difference between the experience they have had with conventional fundraising in other organizations and the much different approach you hope to experience with them, using personalized philanthropy. What would you say? How would they respond or react?

# Chapter Two

## Matrix-Killing Apps of Personalized Philanthropy

### IN THIS CHAPTER

→ If there were really such things, what would holistic gift designs look like?

→ How can "spending rate" gifts acquire the power of twenty?

→ For gift purposes, can you turn a sixty-year-old into an eighty-year-old? (Don't try this at home.)

While many gift, estate, and financial planners have been encouraged to discuss donors' family values, philanthropic objectives, and the emotional aspects of philanthropy, our conventional solicitation models lack tools for translating the donor's big picture into specific gift designs and structures.

Lacking such basic translational gift design tools, our conversations with donors are falling way short. By default, we fall back on the few gift vehicles we have and are easily blinded (even bedazzled?) by their technical beauty. As a result, we treat them as ends in themselves, instead of means.

To fill the void and hopefully restore some creativity to gift planning, I have condensed many examples of gift design experience into three prototypical model designs, game-changers that I sometimes call "killer apps."

In lower tech terms, a killer app might be something like Guttenberg's printing press. Printing the Bible mechanically instead of by hand was disruptive, to say the least. It began a change that resonated through religion and culture. You could think of email as the Internet's

killer app, at least until texting came along, or Facebook, or Twitter. (What's next?)

The applications we'll discuss in this chapter have sometimes been known as a "double ask." That term is confusing and *just plain wrong*: it means asking for an outright gift and a planned gift, yet solely to meet separately-managed annual and planned gift campaign goals. On the other hand, blended or integrative gifts are terms that describe more favorably a single (umbrella-type) gift able to combine multiple gift vehicles toward one purpose.

## Killer App

Wikipedia defines a "killer app" using the jargon of computer programmers and video gamers. It is a computer program that is ingeniously coded or unexpectedly useful— *so necessary that it provides the core value of some larger technology.* For example, the most elegant high-end killer app *software* design substantially increases sales of the *hardware* that supports it.

I think my favorite term for the approaches we'll discuss in this chapter is "killer apps of personalized philanthropy." This brings together the core features of a unique skill set, like no other. Not "planned giving," though it borrows some of the technology. Not "major gifts" or "annual gifts," and certainly not "campaign giving," though its practices may overlap.

Personalized philanthropy is becoming a discipline unto itself:

the disciplined gift-design practice of a new type of planner, perhaps the "enlightened generalist."

## Enter Personalized Philanthropy

*The right gift, for the right donor, for the right purpose, at the right time.* You may have heard this formula expressed as a best practice for gift planners. It is a wonderful mantra to remember, but without some very specific gift applications at hand, it quickly becomes all talk and little action. It is very hard to implement a donor-focused approach in the field if you don't have tools.

Most gift planners, however well-intentioned, have taken a transactional approach to "selling" individual gift vehicles—annual gifts, gift annuities, and bequests, etc.—in order to meet the goals of their corresponding separate fundraising divisions (planned giving, major gifts, capital campaign). While stewardship of donors and writing letters acknowledging the impact of these gifts is, of course, essential, it is often just part of a waiting period until initiating the next gift transaction. However, when you are more engaged in helping the donor shape the big picture of the donor's philanthropy, you have a context for understanding where you are going next, and you are going there together. Each transaction carries more meaning to the donor than just its financial fulfillment. When we talk about *transformation* versus *transaction*, I think this is where the real deal comes from.

Personalized philanthropy, with its donor-focused gift design applications, offers the first real alternative to institution-focused fundraising, and that approach crosses the traditional lines imposed by the siloed organizational structure of many fundraising departments. You'll find that most (and even some of the best) fundraising trainers specialize in and market to one department, and they tend to focus on tactics aimed squarely on advancing one type of gift—planned, major, annual, or capital. They are often training fundraisers to overcome donor objections to the transaction. With only a few exceptions, they rarely present strategic alternatives that would take staff "out of the box" and help them to recognize the donor's big picture. Overcoming objections is most often about push-pull fundraising and convincing someone of something; it's adversarial.

If a donor is truly committed and contributing to an organization, and has been engaged for ten, fifteen, or even thirty years, the donor should have the capability of making *every* kind of gift during that extended time span. Why not address this planning holistically, in the fullness of the commitment, and help donors shape a comprehensive meaningful plan (or something like a master gift agreement) to achieve philanthropic goals, rather than focus on the transaction the institution wants at that particular moment?

### Key Features of the Personalized Philanthropy's Killer Apps

Here are the ten key features of killer apps, in the context of personalized philanthropy:

1. With personalized philanthropy, unlike conventional major or planned gift fundraising, the full spectrum of gifts is on the table for discussion. All the building blocks of philanthropy—both current and future gifts—can be invoked to achieve greater good for donor and institution. Gift plans often integrate current, outright, irrevocable, and revocable commitments.

2. While donors may not be able to achieve the overall philanthropic goal with a single gift, they may reach that goal over time by combining many gifts (outright, life income, and estate) that correspond to individual timing, needs, and assets. Donors often have the capability to go way beyond what they are asked for in an institutional-focused solicitation, but that discussion is never held. *In personalized philanthropy the discovery conversation is central.*

3. Our planning aim, simply stated, is to discover and mesh the compelling interests of the donor with the compelling core

needs of the organization. It is not primarily about selling a gift vehicle, but about understanding and in fact helping to shape the philanthropic goal. However, without specific gift designs and applications well-suited to meet these dual needs, the conversation cannot easily be held. So the development of personalized philanthropy is an evolutionary development, one that will enable next steps that may not have as yet even been imagined.

4. The momentum of the personalized gift process tends to overwhelm or set aside campaign and department silos and impact the fundraising culture, since a gift may simultaneously fulfill goals for multiple fundraising divisions (i.e., annual and endowment). In larger organizations, gift officers collaborate across department boundaries. In smaller organizations, the gift officer may convene a powerful guiding interdisciplinary team of executives, financial, and program officers to figure out how to "get it done." Sometimes, to satisfy a Matrix-like need for order, we could recommend inventing a new category of gift, simply to allow the gift to be acceptable to both divisions, which are normally in competition.

5. Both donor recognition and the startup impact of gifts begin immediately, and grow over time. Recognition includes cumulative lifetime and estate gifts. Program impact and advances are shared and reported frequently, for example, when a faculty member supported by a donor publishes a major paper.

6. Gifts are usually restricted, as opposed to being for general purposes. The use of funds is more clearly tied to the core mission and defining goals of the organization. A challenge for the gift officer is to clearly articulate both core needs that must be met currently and those that need to be met over the long-term, so that restriction language can be properly stated.

7. When gifts are targeted and restricted for a purpose, that means that in a sense they are chained together or harnessed for that purpose. Then, even the smallest gift transactions gain meaning. The smaller gifts can even help drive the larger future

contributions, since they are seen as helping achieve that overarching larger goal. In service of that goal, multiple gifts of many types will be likely, even favored, over time. It is not unusual to combine gift annuities and a bequest with outright gifts. Donors and families can give, each at own their age and stage. No gift is left behind, since in this context, no gift is too small to matter.

## Game-Changing Personalized Gift Apps

*Virtual endowment*—Donor combines and chains together a series of current gifts of a "spending rate" amount that will maintain a program with a future gift (a bequest or other "balloon payment") to endow the program.

*Philanthropic mortgage*—Donor's annual gift commitment covers an amount greater than that needed for maintenance of the program. The "surplus" amount is used to gradually build "equity" in an endowment or a legacy fund until fully established and able to sustain the program for the future.

*Step-up gifts*—Donor establishes a gift at a starting level with an outright gift or, alternatively, "spending rate" annual gifts, and then steps it up, upgrading to a higher level of impact later on, usually through a bequest or other balloon payment, e.g., from a master's scholarship to a doctoral scholarship to a professorial chair.

**definition**

8. Multiyear annual gifts are typically designed to leverage the power of spending rate—annual gifts are planned in combination with legacy/endowment gifts.

9. The solicitation style is less "sell-y," more relationship-based; less push, more the emotional tug and pull of a partnership of discovery and exploration to achieve a shared goal.

10. Gift agreements become an essential part of the process, both for codifying a legally binding commitment and for capturing the entirety of the game plan, spirit, and donative intent. Often a document will include *both* legally binding pledges and revocable commitments. Yet, because discovery and discussion of values have been so central to the process, a donor may regard their gift agreement as much an "ethical will" as a legal contract. This is where personalized

philanthropy and the killer apps excel—in their translational ability to capture the emotional core of the gift as well as the technical vehicles that achieve it.

## The Vastly Underestimated Power of Spending Rate

Each one of these game-changing strategies in one way or another leverages the power of spending rate. The entire point of endowment is to create a stream of annual revenues to maintain program operations. Yet, if it is not possible to obtain the corpus initially, it may still be possible for a donor to provide the stream of annual gifts. In fact, they may already be giving the funds in a less decisive or intentional way.

With this simple approach—focusing on the stream of annual gifts first— many programs can be established that would otherwise never see the light of day. For example, a traditional endowment of $100,000 produces $5,000 of spending, with a 5 percent spending rate. Here is yet another proof that even modest annual gifts (in the context of lifetime and estate giving) can have all the impact and power of major gifts.

If the annual spending commitment precedes the formal establishment of the endowment, who is to say that is not just as valuable as having the endowment itself?

## The Three Matrix-Killing Personalized Philanthropy Gift Applications

In donor-focused gift design, the three model personalized gift applications are virtual endowments, equity building gifts (which are also called philanthropic mortgages), and step-up gifts. These gift designs and prototypes have helped many donors achieve goals beyond what they might have imagined. In the process, they surprised a fair number of fundraising executives because, well, they actually did what they were intended to do: make it possible to raise more and better gifts (no matter how you count them), where both the impact and recognition can begin now. These are the grail of fundraising.

Although there seem to be an infinite variation on these three applications, many of which you may encounter in your own gift practice, let's look at some classic representations of each one.

### Killer App 1: Virtual Endowment

A virtual endowment fills a dual need to provide your organization with funds for operating a core program of your mission up front, and for securing an endowment or legacy fund to sustain it on the back end. The classic example is an older donor, in her eighties, who wanted to support stem cell research, but could not make the outright gift of $1 million needed to establish the endowment gift the institution was requesting.

The donor's advisor asked her to consider that she could not use the full charitable deduction for the gift, or might possibly need to retain the asset during her lifetime. However, she did have other sources of income available for current giving.

As an alternative to making the outright gift of the full amount to establish an endowment, the donor was able to make a commitment to giving annual gifts of $50,000 each year for the rest of her life, estimated to be around ten years. Both the donor and her advisor were comfortable about establishing a bequest as a separate and distinct gift of the $1 million through her estate.

We developed an umbrella plan that included two gifts, linked together with a single gift agreement: (1) the multiyear pledge for annual gifts based on her years of life expectancy, and (2) a separate pledge or contract to include a gift in her will as a bequest of $1 million.

For many years, this donor had been a health care activist during the time stem cell research was not widely permitted in the United States. She truly enjoyed supporting the vital research that was so important to her. She met the researchers and celebrated the gift with them.

Knowing that her irrevocable pledge for the legacy gift would be fulfilled on her demise, she was fully recognized by the organization during her lifetime. The essential stem cell program could be funded immediately and the researchers had assurance of future funding. Thus, both the impact of her gift and its recognition in our campaign could begin immediately.

The "virtual" part of the endowment meant that each of her annual gifts could be treated as if it were the 5 percent spending on a $1 million endowment. That meant that each gift would be fully expended in the year given until, upon her demise, the proceeds would be used to create an actual endowment fund in her name.

## Key Features of the Virtual Endowment

◆ A loyal donor with a pattern of annual giving, who also has a bequest in mind (a known expectancy), along with a compelling desire to have greater impact and recognition, both starting now.

◆ A gift agreement that includes a future balloon payment (usually a bequest) to insure that the annual gifts will continue; irrevocable pledge of the bequest or balloon payment would likely be required for recognition during donor's lifetime.

◆ Organizational policies that treat the gift as a unit and the agreement as an umbrella, and thus which enable designating of the annual spending amount and the ultimate endowment spending to be chained together and used toward the same purpose. If so, the program could begin immediately and the donor may be recognized for the full commitment.

### A Virtual Chair for the Chair Emeritus

A former chairman of the organization wanted to make a significant and meaningful gift to support new scientists' careers, by designating a minimum sum expected from an Individual Retirement Account (IRA). The donor was comfortably able to make a pledge that would be guaranteed by his estate, knowing the IRA gift would ultimately be larger than the pledge. This gift would help provide new scientists—a different one every few years—with a substantial start up package, to help them build and equip new laboratories until they were fully established and able to apply for competitive grants. This arrangement, which is a core and continuing need, is often called a career-development chair.

While the donor knew his gift would be created upon his demise, he faced great disappointment because he would be unable to meet the incumbents of "his" chair. He realized, however, that for many years he had been making annual gifts that were very close to the amount that would ultimately be produced by his endowment, once it was funded. If the career development chair costs $750,000, it would be expected to produce annual support in the range of $37,500 each year. Since the donor's pattern of giving was already so close to this amount, he is seriously considering designating that his annual gift be used for that purpose. When that happens, the career development chair will be able to start up immediately, and he will meet his first incumbent.

While preparing the final notes for this section, I'm so pleased to report that this gift happened the way the donor envisioned it. During the early years, the scientists' research will be supported by the annual gifts; during the later years, by the spending from the bequest. The multiyear annual gifts were not the complete answer, of course, but they enabled the donor to see the beneficial impact of his philanthropy during his lifetime and, it seems, they also created a kind of moral imperative for the donor to chain the current and future gifts together to assure the full program.

Obviously, such classic cases are well-suited for older donors. But the terms can be flexible, once the concepts are understood. It would be great if, at least for the purposes of planning a gift, you could turn an eighty-year-old into a sixty-year-old. It's almost possible with some of the variations we will explore further.

### In Memoriam Virtual Endowment

Planners like to see what happens when you try to implement a new idea in the field—does it just look good on paper or does it really get results?

That's what Cynthia O'Donnell and I wanted to know when we combined forces in 2005 to test the virtual endowment in the field. She learned about the "killer apps" and, driven by curiosity, wanted to see for herself if they might apply in her own shop. Nothing makes a more compelling case than success, such as the one described in this article about a donor who established a virtual endowment at Morristown Medical Center.

### $1.3 Million Endows Fellowship at Breast Center

A former New Jersey resident, Edward Reid, permanently endowed the Lois A. Reid Fellowship in Breast Imaging by generously giving $1.3 million to The Carol W. and Julius A. Rippel Breast Center in memory of his wife, Lois. The Lois A. Reid Endowment Fund in Breast Imaging funds one fellow each year to initiate new trials and medical advances in breast cancer detection and care.

Previously, the donor also funded a new digital mammography machine, making Morristown Medical Center one of the first all digital centers in Morris County.

"The donor was aware of the importance of state-of-the-art equipment," says Dr. Paul Friedman, medical director of the Rippel Breast Center. "But he even saw beyond the equipment needs to also invest in training."

Both the hospital and the donor recognized the shortage in skilled radiologists who perform breast imaging. Thus the idea was born of creating a fellowship in breast imaging. "If you don't have the proper manpower, then all the machines in the world won't find cancer," says Dr. Friedman. "You need the brain power to interpret and analyze the mammograms."

Mr. Reid created a virtual endowment in 2011 by planning to make an annual gift of $65,000 a year for life and then having his estate, through a bequest, pay the $1.3 million upon his death, permanently funding the endowment. The donor was recognized at the time the gift was made. Subsequently, he received some unexpected funds and paid the endowment in full.

"While a true endowment requires 100 percent funding up front, a virtual endowment requires annual payments and a signed estate intention that will come to fruition after the donor's death," says Cynthia W. O'Donnell, JD, director of gift planning at the Foundation. "A virtual endowment functions like a fully funded endowment, with annual income paid to the charity and the donor receiving recognition for the entire value of the gift during his lifetime."

## Killer App 2: Building Philanthropic Equity (Like a Mortgage)

How do you even begin to explain the idea of building philanthropic equity? We originally called this gift a "philanthropic mortgage," but that term can go in and out of favor during a financial downturn. With the real estate market back up, at least for now, it seems okay to talk about it again.

When you buy your home, you can pay for it over time. You don't have to wait to move in until it's fully paid for. Why not apply this familiar concept to philanthropic giving? It's the idea of *building equity in your endowment fund.* Instead of waiting until your pledge is completed, with each of your regular payments you are building equity.

Let's say that you were fortunate to receive financial support that made it possible for you to attend college, and so one of your life's ambitions would be to create your own professorial chair at your college to give back in a meaningful way. When you visit the campus, you could see "your professor," knowing you helped your university substantially.

In a classic situation, under a plan that builds equity in your endowment (philanthropic mortgage), part of each payment goes to cover the annual maintenance costs of operating the chair; the remainder of the payment goes for endowment. When fully funded, the program is self-sustaining. This is a true philanthropic partnership between the donor and the organization.

This is exactly what my friend, Robert King, then Director of Leadership and Planned Gifts at Knox College, and I discussed when he described his work with a very promising supporter. Since Knox is also my alma mater, Robert was "my" planned giving officer, and we enjoy getting together.

We talked about how the idea of a philanthropic mortgage might apply in the case of a prospective gift by a Microsoft retiree who dearly wanted to fund a professorial chair. He was not prepared to make the outright gift of a million dollars, but looked forward even less to wading through ten years of pledge payments before meeting the first incumbent of his chair.

Steven—Yes, this was the gift that was able to take advantage of a "philanthropic mortgage." It's a seven-year commitment funded with $200,000 up front and annual payments of $160,000. The donors were very pleased that they would be able to meet the professor who will hold the chair next year rather than having to wait ten years as originally anticipated.

—Robert King, Director Planned Gifts, Knox College, Galesburg, Illinois

*(From the desk of Robert King, Esq.)*

❝Over the 40 years since graduation, I have come to view my Knox education as the "launching pad" that set the trajectory for the rest of my professional life. My Knox education provided me with the flexibility and the agility to adapt to the significant social and technological changes that have occurred in my life by teaching me how to think, not what to think.

At Knox, I also met the person who would become my mentor and role model, Professor Wayne Green, who exhibited compassion and generosity towards his students that I will never forget. One of my favorite memories of Professor Green was the time he found me and my classmate Dick Fritz '66 in a physics lab trying in vain to make an instrument work. This was after we had pulled an all-nighter during BETA pledge week. Professor Green went back to his office, brought back two small cushions, cleared off areas on two lab benches, took away the instrument, closed the window shades, turned off the lights, and said he'd be back in a few hours.

Professor Green also provided Dick and me with a useful work philosophy that has stuck with us ever since—'First, try a minimal approach. If that doesn't work, just use a bigger hammer.'

As I approached my retirement from a successful career in the computer industry, I started looking for ways to help Knox. I especially wanted my gift to have an impact on current and future students. As my wife, Maria, and I worked with Robert King, senior director of gift planning, on the general mechanics of an endowment, we learned that Knox was planning to add earth sciences back into its curriculum. We immediately committed to funding the Douglas and Maria Bayer Chair in Earth Sciences.

The professor who fills this position will have the potential to help address one of the most relevant worldwide problems, global environmental deterioration, while also having a positive influence on future Knox students much as Professor Green influenced me.❞

—Douglas Bayer '66

> ### Key Features of an Equity-Building Gift
>
> ◆ Donor contributes the spending rate, and more.
>
> ◆ Payments cover both annual maintenance and incrementally grow the endowment.
>
> ◆ The endowment is self-sustaining when fully funded.
>
> ◆ The payment schedule is flexible, including the number of years and payments; includes down payment.
>
> ◆ Chair named immediately.
>
> ◆ The "mortgage" agreement is established with an irrevocable and bookable pledge.
>
>

With Bob's help, the donor found a way to make his gift. He made an initial down payment, with subsequent payments that would cover both the spending rate and build equity to endow a chair. He was able to name the chair and provide some needed support right away. He and his family had the unexpected joy and pleasure of meeting the incumbent of their chair ten years *sooner* than they at first anticipated.

Why didn't Bob consider a Virtual Endowment for this donor? No way was a donor in his fifties going to be making payments of any amount for the rest of his long life. But, through this strategy of *building equity while maintaining the annual costs*, he was able to accelerate his gift and have it begin immediately. This arrangement opened up a path beyond conventional giving. The donor was able to apply a financial strategy he well understood and used his good business sense to realize his philanthropic goal now, rather than much later.

### Killer App 3: Step-Up the Impact of Your Gift

So many donors have adopted this ingenious approach of upgrading their impact over the years, it is difficult to pick the best one to illustrate. There are almost an infinite number of ways to combine gifts as building blocks, once you know what you are trying to achieve. Here are just a few techniques I have helped donors to use:

> ◆ If you have been making annual gifts on a regular basis for general purposes, one way to step-up your gift is simply to

promise to continue that good habit on a multiyear basis; *and* you can also restrict your gifts for something specific that's important to you.

◆ You can step-up the impact of your gift by adding more to your endowment, if you have one, either during your lifetime through your estate. Or, if you have already been making annual gifts for

a long time and you don't have an endowment, you could step-up your support by committing to establish one later through your estate plan.

◆ If you have a number of charitable gift annuities, you could dedicate the remainder to a specific purpose important to you. Many donors add a bequest to increase the total.

◆ If you already have an endowment in your will for something important, you can start making current lifetime gifts for that same purpose. Why should you have to wait for your program to begin until after you die? Plus, expending the full amount of your annual gift gives you more bang for your buck. This multiyear series of annual gifts, combined with your later bequest, is like a virtual endowment. This is how even modest gifts can make a difference. Add a gift annuity to sweeten up the endowment fund even more, if receiving the fixed annual payments is important to you or a spouse.

◆ You can step-up the impact of your gift simply by increasing the number of years or the number of dollars that you have already committed to your multiyear annual gift. If you need to make required distributions from your IRA, and you don't need all the income, you're probably more than half way there.

### A Gift that Steps Up, More than Once

A long-standing annual donor and friend of our organization very close to my heart had a great but seemingly unreachable goal to establish a professorial chair in memory of her first husband, a doctor who had died from lung cancer. The chair could possibly be established with a bequest for $1.5 million, but that seemed very far removed from her reality. However, by combining resources, she and her daughters found they were able to establish an endowment fund for a relatively modest amount each. Their fund was used to support a Masters scholarship for a total gift of $150,000.

To achieve her goal, the donor pledged that upon her demise she would make a bequest that would be used to add to the endowment fund and step it up to the higher level of the professorial chair. In prior years, too, the donor had established charitable gift annuities and a charitable remainder trust, and they were able to designate that the proceeds of these could also be added to the fund for the chair. Finally, in honor of her then-current husband, she made an additional gift from her estate to create a research fund that could be used to enhance the research of the future incumbent of their chair.

This gift integrated many types of gifts—that might have been seen as transactional—into building blocks

#### How to Count It

Because the essential elements of the agreement were backed by an irrevocable pledge, the gift was recognized fully during the lifetime of the donor, to her (and our) great delight. Other ingredients included charitable gift annuities, whose proceeds would ultimately be added to the endowment fund. On financial statements, only the charitable portion was recorded as an asset, but the entire transfer for the annuity was captured at face value on our Total Financial Resource Development reporting (more about that in **Chapter Five**).

practical tip

## Umbrella Gifts and the Spend—Powerful Allies

The "killer apps" of personalized philanthropy each employ a powerful tool that you might call umbrella gifts. They are simple to understand, but sometimes difficult to describe. Umbrella gifts utilize various building blocks of philanthropy as elements with different functions which activate at different times, but that all share the common purpose and advance the "why" and "what for" of the gift. And all the killer apps are powered by annual gifts of the "spend."

to achieve an important objective over a number of years. Yet the impact began right away. The donor enjoyed a relationship with the scholarship student, while knowing that the family professorial chair would be created in future years.

## A Donor Story

One donor was especially important in shaping my thinking about personalized philanthropy. Susan Green was a tough and edgy donor, a strong and successful woman; yet no one realized her giving potential. How was I to know that she was going to change my life? That change started on the day she decided that she wanted to create an endowment fund for scientists whose work was so curiosity-driven and so new that it might not yet even have a name.

Susan simply "didn't love" any of the proposals we offered. In the course of time, we proposed most of the standard vehicles to her. We looked at proposals to support students and young scientists. We proposed funding research for every kind of project and disease you could name. Finally, we realized she didn't want something with a name. She knew what she DID want, and we didn't have it "on the shelf."

Susan wanted to fund scientists who had a dream, whose heads others might think were in the clouds, and whose research was not ready for prime-time grant consideration. She wanted to be their patron benefactor.

They were her kind of people, and she was their kind of people. Since it was completely true that we didn't have anything like this, we agreed that somehow, together, we would create it. And we did.

It still seems unthinkable that even fifteen years ago, when Susan's story began, such an essential and defining core need of the Weizmann Institute of Science did not have its own specific "bucket" of funds. After all, the Institute's core mission had always been built around people pursuing basic science, rather than specific applications, cures, and engineering solutions. The Weizmann Institute's culture may be its greatest innovation and achievement, providing a model of energetic collaboration, driven from the bottom up by multidisciplinary teams, amid total academic freedom.

With Susan, there were arguments—some heated. I never had a relationship with a donor that was so turbulent, but ultimately so satisfying. I still have Susan's notes and cross-outs on our first drafts. I wanted to call this the "cutting-edge" fund to reflect the out-of-box scientific ideas being explored. But Susan thought that sounded too much like hedge-fund; it didn't catch what *she* meant. She even threatened (or rather, politely asserted) that she would refuse to put her name on it and not make the gift. Finally, she suggested "Discovery," and it stuck. She hoped many others would follow her. Now, alongside of all those research funds for cancer, MS, alternative energy, feeding the planet, and so on, *there would be a fund for science so new it did not have a name.*

## Funding Discovery through Personalized Philanthropy

What we'd been through to get us that far brought us closer. Now that we were onto a discussion about funding, everything was on the table for discussion. It wasn't the usual solicitation, where you make a pitch for something your organization wants to sell, ask for an amount (would you consider a gift of x?), and then wait in silence for your donor to speak. It was a conversation unlike any I had ever had, focused on the donor's most compelling interest, which also happened to be a compelling (and largely unmet) need of the organization.

It went something like this. In essence, Susan had several pockets, some holding current funds and some future. There was a potential source for annual gifts: Susan had been donating cash for years to a donor advised fund. There was some money built up in that fund, and more ready to go there or someplace else. She also revealed that there was a more substantial source of funds possible for an estate gift, from a retirement fund—an IRA. Susan was so invested in the vision of the Discovery Endowment Fund that everything was on the table.

## Celebration . . . and a Glitch

Susan decided to sign an agreement, backed by a pledge, that a series of annual gifts would establish the Discovery Endowment Fund, and that the IRA would be designated for the fund on her demise. We celebrated that gift as a shared achievement.

For several years, we ran the fund this way, happily. Until the glitch. Susan was holding up her end of the deal, making fairly substantial annual gifts that were growing the endowment. But the amount that was actually being sent to scientists in support of their Discovery research—our endowment spending rate—seemed so slight to Susan that *she* felt the impact of her gift was negligible.

Once again, we put our heads together, and Susan decided she wanted to make a major shift in strategy. As generous as her individual annual gifts were, her eventual IRA gift would be much larger. We realized that by itself, that single gift from her estate would be more than twenty times her annual gifts. In the future, this would create a viable endowment, one that would be able to produce an amount each year that was at least as much as the annual gifts she had been giving and intended to keep giving during her lifetime.

We settled on a plan that would produce the most bang for the buck now, and also take into account the entirety of Susan's future plans. We decided to consider the result if each of the annual gifts was fully expendable in the year it was given. There was no point in designating them for endowment now, when the future gift would more than sustain the pace of annual gifts Susan was making during her lifetime.

Upon the realization that expendable gifts could be combined with endowment gifts as part of a *unified plan,* we agreed to reclassify the gifts she had given over the years from endowment to expendable, so they could be fully utilized for Discovery research and have impact right now. And we designated future estate gifts towards the legacy that would provide

## What Counts and How You Count It

*Counting the annual gifts:* In the early days of this giving program, for financial purposes in our campaign the yearly gifts counted as they were received each year. Why not count the string of annual gifts committed? Because in this case, they were contributions from a donor-advised fund. Such gifts cannot be used to fulfill legal pledges. Our gift agreement included a provision that the donor intended to make these gifts and would recommend them, but this was not a legally binding provision. Note, however, that in our total financial resource development reports (explained in **Chapter Five**), we were able to record the entire five-year set of "expected gifts" as revocable commitments.

*Counting long-term commitments:* Our donor had included a provision that her IRA would come to our organization, so we and she knew the long-term future of her program would be assured. She felt so confident that this gift would, in fact, be received that she was comfortable signing an irrevocable pledge that would be binding on her estate, and that could be satisfied by funds from her IRA or other assets.

### Example

annual support of the research long into the future. The current gifts would essentially behave as if the endowment fund had already been created. Each gift in the long series of annual contributions would have an impact much greater, because it would be fully expendable.

Imagine how the power of the gift is amplified if the endowment spending rate were 5 percent. That would mean that each annual gift in the series has an impact of twenty times that amount, compared to a one-off gift. For example, if the annual gift were $50,000, that would be the equivalent of having a $1 million endowment that was producing spending of 5 percent. Our thinking about multiyear annual gifts and endowment gifts was beginning to change radically.

The unified and holistic plan for funding discovery produced some interesting benefits, which might not otherwise have happened. First, there was immediate recognition of the donor and enhanced impact upon the program, because of the nature of the annual gifts. The multiyear gifts that were coming from the donor-advised fund—even though they would count in our Total Financial Resource Development numbers—could only be booked financially each year, as they arrived. However, with the addition of the legally binding estate commitment, the contribution value of the gift on our books was considered very significant. The donor could be recognized in our most elite giving circle, and the gift helped our overall campaign success in that year. Finally, the donor was very engaged in helping to share the news of this special new fund to support the core need of Discovery research at the institute.

Over the years, so many donors have opted to make gifts for curiosity-driven research because they relate personally to Susan's goal to be a patron donor for scientists who are reaching for the farthest star. Her Discovery Fund has been cited many times by scientists as their dream gift. For me, it represented a personal origin story of the virtual endowment, a model since used many times to blend current and future gifts.

## To Recap

◆ Personalized philanthropy starts with the donor's goal for mission impact that begins now and grows over time, not with vehicles. The three killer apps—virtual endowments, philanthropic mortgages, and step-up gifts—are model strategies to reach the goal.

◆ In any of the killer apps, the traditional transactional gift vehicles—bequests, gift annuities, pledges for annual gifts, etc.—can all be used as building blocks, tied together with a gift agreement.

◆ Think about spending rate. The "spend" powers the killer apps. It is the oft-overlooked raison d'être for endowment gifts in the first place. The spending rate, in a personalized gift design, becomes a virtual endowment—the annual distribution from what will become a fully-funded endowment. It is key to "chaining" together the modest current expendable gifts with future endowment gifts. Smart donors and advisors will soon recognize and learn how to use the spend as a way of increasing their impact and having recognition begin now. Keep an eye on spending rate: it's one of the things that will change how philanthropy is done.

# Chapter Three

## Radically Rethinking Endowment: Powerful Examples in Practice

### IN THIS CHAPTER

---→ Can some familiar building blocks of philanthropy substitute for endowment?

---→ How might you turn a traditional endowment "upside down"?

---→ Is it possible to reconfigure the boundaries of classic annual, major, and planned gifts?

A few years ago, I wrote a riff on a great classic parable. My insight came while rereading the story of "The Four Children," that part of the traditional celebration of the Jewish Passover service known as the Seder, which talks about four types of individuals—their personalities, their learning styles.

Passover is the holiday that commemorates in story and song the end of the enslavement of the Jews by Pharaoh in Egypt—the Exodus. The term *Seder* literally refers to "the order of things" for the annual retelling of the story. For Jews and many others, this story of the Exodus is an inspiration about how both individuals and peoples come by their identities. And for me, always on a quest for order, it was a turning point in my thinking about personalized philanthropy.

It occurred to me that the four children in the story were almost exact analogies of four donor personalities I so often encounter. (Okay, there *are* a few twists.) Now, there are so many systems for donor profiling that you can hardly keep track of them. They are almost all good, and so often the characters *all* resonate for me, but I can never remember them. For one thing, there are always more than four. But, the four children? I

already know them. My colleagues like to joke that for me, everything is like Passover. It's no use arguing; there is something to that.

What is so distinctive about "The Four Children" (and the thing that makes this a parable) is that the story actually teaches us something. It prescribes meeting the children where they are and suggests a specific way of engaging with each type.

Not only did the four children's personalities resonate so strongly for me because they were familiar analogies to my donors, but because they also connected these different personalities—an approach I realized I had been following with donors for many years.

The story of the Seder introduces us to four children—the Wise, the Wicked, the Simple, and the one who doesn't know how to ask. The essence is that while there may be one truth and one path for every person, we should not use a standardized, unvarying approach for all types of donors but must tailor our words and method to conform to each type of donor.

**Meeting Donors Where They Are**

The core idea of the parable "The Four Children" is that a personalized kind of engagement with each individual is likely to have the most beneficial outcome. We intuitively know this, somehow, but there are plenty of others who feel a single prescribed and unwavering answer is best for everyone.

## The Four Children of the Passover Story
### What Do They Ask?

*Wise*—Immersed in the letter and spirit of the laws, driven to curiosity, the wise child asks: "Will you tell me more so I can do more?"

*Wicked*—Has wisdom to understand, but because the rituals seem lacking personal meaning, may become more reserved or even disinterested. Asks: "What does all this have to do with *me*?"

*Simple*—Overwhelmed by the magnitude of ritual, the simple child asks: "What is this all about?"

*The child who does not know how to ask*—This child, naïve, uncertain and intellectually curious, cannot figure how form a question. It is up to us to ask on their behalf: "Where can we begin?"

What is the challenge that each the four children present to their elders? In the sidebar I provide a shorthand description.

While the idea of engaging *children* "where they are" sounds simple, but seen in the light of experience there is certainly more to it than at first thought. And when it comes to helping *donors* make major philanthropic decisions, mixing the financial, the personal, and the philanthropic can become complicated pretty quickly.

Reflecting on donor personalities I suddenly began to rethink the standard questions and answers. Observing and respecting the trajectory of each donor, since each donor starts in a different place, they may end up in a different place.

And so, I began to think of The Four Donors as distinct yet related personalities. I wondered what it would be like to consider some of the innate processes that characterize donors when they are considering charitable action. Here's my present thinking about just some of the dimensions that each donor can present and a sense of their mind-set when approaching philanthropic questions.

The Four Philanthropic Donors—
How Do We Characterize Them?

*Wise*—Astute, aware, careful, clever, discerning, thoughtful. "I'm in."

*Wicked*—Reserved, mischievous, competent, expert, adept, able, questioning. "I'm out."

*Simple*—Straightforward, uncomplicated, sincere, trusting, direct. "I haven't thought about that question."

*Does not know how to ask*—Naive, curious, inquisitive, searching. "I didn't know one could ask questions."

### *The Four Donors*

In the Passover Seder, "The Four Children" offers a lesson on meeting people *where* they are and appreciating them for *who* they are. Each of the four donors helps translate our charitable inclination and personalities into action in a different way. Personalized philanthropy is about finding just the right gift for the right person at just the right time.

I've come up with my own version of "The Four Children," which I call "The Four Donors." It's a "parable" about choosing the right gift, for the right donor, at the right time, and meeting donors where they are.

**The Wise Donors** *(Astute, aware, careful, clever, discerning, thoughtful)— These are the wise and loyal annual donors who give without being asked, perhaps even every year. We meet wise donors right where they are. We thank them for the gifts they have been making. Because they give every year and are wise, they are eager and curious to hear about* *ways they can increase the impact of their annual gift, even without changing one bit their regular habit of giving, at first. For instance, when they commit to a series of annual gifts, each gift in the series can have up to twenty times the impact of a solitary gift (based on a spending rate of 5 percent). When the time is right, they'll want to hear about other annual donors, like them, who established bequests and achieved an impact from their gift far beyond what they might have imagined possible.*

**The Wicked Donors** *Reserved, mischievous, competent, expert, adept, able, questioning)—These donors are not really wicked, but simply reserved. They give, but also need to receive something in return. There's a give and take. We meet these donors right where they are; perhaps they are feeling slightly insecure. We can suggest a new way to give, through a charitable gift annuity, to assure them of receiving payments each year for their lifetime. As they grow more assured about their own income, they are intrigued to hear that some donors establish an annuity every year, with some having a dozen or more. Enjoying this security, a surprising number of annuitants become annual donors, by contributing some of the income they don't need, year after year. Because they feel so invested, they are also pleased to learn that many annuity donors have made bequests, which turn out to be much larger than any gifts they could make during their lifetime.*

**The Simple Donors** *(Straightforward, uncomplicated, sincere, trusting, direct)—With simple donors, tradition rules and a bequest is the gift they begin and sometimes end with. They come to see their gift as something larger than just themselves. They often chose the same form of giving as their parents, saying as my parent planted before me, so do I plant for my (charitable) children. We meet these donors right where they are and thank them for their gift intention, telling them that from bequests often come the largest and most significant contributions. Some bequest donors feel a need to assure themselves of the certainty of their ultimate gift, and they may seek ways to make a secure pledge of their gift. Bequest donors are often the most ardent supporters we have, and some are only too happy to begin making a modest annual gift, perhaps to start up a scholarship during their lifetime with spending rate gifts, knowing their gift of greatest significance will come later.*

**The Naïve Donors** *(curious, inquisitive, questioning, searching)—The naïve donors are most rare: donors who do not know how to act on their charitable impulse. They "don't know how to ask," perhaps in the sense that while they may be very successful financially and worldly-wise, they are not familiar with the conventions of philanthropy. They may have* *no idea of what a pledge is. Or, they may have inherited great wealth and feel overwhelmed now at becoming the steward of a parent's or a sibling's or even a child's legacy. They may have the smartest advisors and feel a great drive to give, but have no idea about how or even what to give for. That these individuals turn to you should be regarded as a great privilege. Meet these donors where they are, and listen for what is important to them, not to you. Be a discerning listener, for they bring a worthy challenge to help begin an important philanthropic journey.*

The idea of gift officers meeting donors where they are sounds simple, if you have an ounce of sensitivity. What is not so simple is what to do next.

Having reflected for so long on this idea of four types of donor personalities, I suddenly began to rethink the whole idea of endowment as the be-all and end-all of philanthropic planning, the singularity.

Radically rethinking means that if each donor starts in a different place, each may end up in different places. You have a chance for a much better charitable gift if you *pay attention to the donors' places and trajectories,* not only yours.

And you need to have a different answer for each questioner, depending on where they begin.

But, before we look closely at endowment, and scholarships in particular, let's step back and take a look at those four donor personalities that drove all this radical rethinking.

## Focusing on a Critical Core Need: Scholarships

Fundraisers and philanthropists seem intuitively to "get" scholarships. While we all think we have a good idea how an endowed scholarship should be established and how it should work, you can achieve much more than you might have thought: seeing scholarships in the light of personalized philanthropy, *from a completely different angle,* can turn conventional endowment design on its head. While the idea of endowment can help crack the door to major gifts, these personally designed gift apps kick it in and knock it down.

So, this chapter is full of donor stories, examples, and strategies devoted to scholarships and what might be a radical new way to look at endowment design. Ultimately, I think this approach to shaping endowment gifts will become commonplace and be considered a best practice. But for now, it is new. Clearly, you can substitute other core needs in place of scholarships. If your organization does not desire endowments, because the focus is most properly placed on satisfying immediate needs, like food, shelter, or clothing, this approach might suggest an alternative or substitute for endowment; a renewable resource, something akin to building board-designated quasi-endowment or cash reserves for an organization in need of financial stability.

### *Identifying Core Needs in both Large and Small Organizations*

Why is radically rethinking endowment so critical for you, especially if you work in a small organization and even if you do not have "scholarships," per se? Every organization has core needs—sometimes we call them "evergreen" needs—as well as immediate needs and priorities.

By core needs, I mean those that really define the mission when a donor asks, "What do you need the money for?" It might not be as easy as you think to name them, and it helps to walk around your organization with an open mind and eye to see what is going on there. In my own organization, we developed a grid that could be used to match our vital programs with donors' needs. I found that each one of the vital programs would resonate with a certain kind of donor. If I listened first, I could find a close match:

### Identifying Core Needs

| What we call it... | How donors think of it... |
| --- | --- |
| Discovery Fund | Science so new it doesn't have a name; cutting-edge basic curiosity-driven research. |

## Identifying Core Needs

| What we call it... | How donors think of it... |
| --- | --- |
| Research Fund | Cancer, neuroscience, genetic diseases, energy, and more, that most people are familiar with. |
| New Scientist Fund and Career Development | Recruit and encourage outstanding young researchers. |
| President's Contingency Fund | Provide a permanent source of funding for pressing needs as chosen by the president. |
| Scholarship Funds | Endow Masters or Doctoral Scholarship, or Post-Doctoral Fellowship. |
| Professional Chair | Support the career of a prominent scientist. |

Think of it this way: if we had a very large endowment that could take care of all our annual needs, what are the mission-critical goals we would meet today with that money? Donors may ask this question at the moment they realize they can make a much larger gift than they thought possible. You need to help them draw their own link between your long-term existence and your everyday mission—the connection between their most compelling and driving interest and your compelling need. It may not  be as easy as you might think, since fundraising for annual, capital, or endowment gifts does not often specify what these needs are (except the need to make an annual gift, for example), so sometimes it is surprisingly hard to mesh the needs of donors and the charities they care about. You need more than the general case statement. There has to be a case statement for *that* donor and the use of *that donor's* funds.

There are many cases where personalized gift designs can both power and empower major gifts that could not otherwise have happened. Each in

## Game-Changing Personalized Gift Apps

Before going to specific cases, let's quickly review the three "classic" game-changing personalized gift strategies and how you might deploy them for scholarships right in the trenches, in real situations with real donors.

*Power of Spending Rate*

1. *Virtual endowment*—Donor combines and chains together a series of current gifts of a "spending rate" amount that will maintain a program with a future gift (a bequest or other "balloon payment") to endow the program.

2. *Philanthropic mortgage*—Donor's annual gift commitment covers an amount greater than that need for maintenance of the program. The "surplus" amount is used to gradually build "equity" in an endowment or a legacy fund until fully established and able to sustain the program for the future.

3. *Step-up gifts*—Donor establishes a gift at a starting level with an outright gift or, alternatively, current "spending rate" annual gifts, and then steps it up, upgrading to a higher level of impact later on, usually through a bequest or other balloon payment, e.g., from a master's scholarship to a doctoral scholarship to a professorial chair.

The vastly under-estimated power of spending rate—Each one of these game-changing strategies in one way or another leverages the power of spending rate. The entire point of endowment is to create a stream of annual revenues to maintain program operations. Yet, if it is not possible to obtain the corpus initially, it may still be possible for a donor to provide the stream of annual gifts. In fact, they may already be giving the funds in a less decisive or intentional way.

With this simple approach—focusing on the stream of annual gifts first—many programs can be established that would otherwise never see the light of day. For example, a traditional endowment of $100,000 produces $5,000 of spending, with a 5 percent spending rate. Here is yet another proof that even modest annual gifts (in the context of lifetime and estate giving) can have all the impact and power of major gifts.

If the annual spending commitment precedes the formal establishment of the endowment, who is to say that is not just as valuable as having the endowment itself?

definition

its own way represents a kind of ideal for fundraising, chaining together current and future gifts that support current needs and secure future needs. Here are a few examples of scholarships that have come about, or have been upgraded, by "meeting the donors where they are" with personalized philanthropy.

## Scholarship with Virtual Endowment: Turning Endowment on Its Head

A Wise donor, indeed. Arthur is a loyal annual donor. He generally makes a gift every year from his personal foundation, almost without being asked, and he designates his gifts for general funds. Starting there, with the annual gifts, Arthur eagerly responded to opportunities for increased impact.

From his pattern of regular annual giving, it was clear that Arthur was not ready to part with a large contribution at this time. He had been making gifts for so many years and was very comfortable with his habit of annual giving. However, in an extended conversation, we found that given the opportunity to have a greater impact with little or no change in his annual giving patterns, Arthur would happily make two new choices. He decided for the first time that he wanted to restrict his gifts, and he determined he would designate them for a scholarship. His regular annual gifts would go much farther as a series than as individual gifts. In fact, with no change, his annual gift would perfectly support an annual scholarship.

For the years in which Arthur would continue to make annual gifts, he would have a virtual endowment. His annual gift of $7,500, when viewed as part of a scholarship series, would have the power of a gift 20 times larger, since $7,500 equals a 5 percent spending rate from a $150,000 endowment. Funding a long-running program with these multiyear annual gifts essentially turns endowment on its head. The focus and driver has become the repeated annual gifts, rather than the single gift of principal.

Along with his enthusiasm for continuing the tried and true pattern of continuing annual gifts, Arthur was also perfectly willing to pledge that at a future point, on his death or possibly sooner, he would contribute through his foundation an outright gift or balloon payment that would fully fund his scholarship, so that it would continue in future years. At that point, a virtual endowment becomes a true endowment. In the meantime, Arthur's scholarship would start up immediately and would be recognized now, and his scholarship student would be named right away.

### Immediate Impact

Arthur's total gift plan included a multiyear commitment for annual gifts, along with a separate commitment for the balloon payment (bequest). The two aspects were each secured by a legally binding pledge, and so the entire combined gift was counted in the year the pledge was signed. And, later, if he decides his foundation can make a larger gift than originally contemplated, his master's scholarship could be upgraded to a doctoral scholarship or postdoctoral fellowship, or even a professorial chair.

**observation**

## From Postdoc to Philanthropist: A Classic Endowed Scholarship, Stepped Up

Wicked or not? Better to think of this donor as reserved and questioning. The most effective donors have often learned to think with the head, not just their heart. Donors who need to receive as well as give certainly aren't wicked. They just need a sense of security and smart financial planning that allows them to explore options for increasing their gifts to reach ambitious goals.

Richard was a postdoc thirty years before he became a philanthropist. ("Postdoc" is slang for an individual holding a doctoral degree who is engaged in a temporary period of mentored research and/or scholarly training for the purpose of acquiring the professional skills needed to pursue a chosen career path.) While a student, he developed a new process for freezing protein crystals, reducing protein analysis from six to twelve months to just a couple of hours. This process became standard practice in laboratories all over the world. But Richard left academia to pursue a career in business, and as a result did not become aware of his impact on basic science until many years later. Richard and his wife wanted someone else to have the same opportunities they had. He says, "When success came, we made a list of all the things we wanted to do for the rest of our lives, and giving back was right near the top." They decided to create a scholarship.

This scholarship started out as an outright contribution to establish an endowment fund, based on their success in business. You know how it works. That fund would spin out an annual spending rate or distribution that creates many scholars in their name over the years to come (e.g., if the endowment for the scholarship costs an outright contribution of $150,000 and the spending rate is 5 percent, the scholarship would be expected to spin off or distribute $7,500 per year, funding many students over the years.)

Several years after creating, with an outright contribution, that classic scholarship at the masters' level, they decided they wanted to augment it. However, they were not able to make another large outright contribution to move from one level to another. As an alternative, they obtained a charitable gift annuity. The gift annuity immediately gave them the assurance that their fund would grow in future years, increasing the impact of their scholarship. Of course, it also provided them an income tax charitable deduction in the year of the gift and then a stream of lifetime payments for the rest of their lives.

After their deaths, the remaining proceeds will be added to their scholarship fund, helping it step up to the higher postdoc level. It seems likely they will find other ways to add to the impact of their scholarship fund over a productive and philanthropic lifetime. It is possible their masters could move to a doctoral scholarship or a postdoctoral fellowship, or even a professorial chair. In our organization, donors frequently use charitable gift annuities, combining them with bequests and outright gifts to establish major philanthropic funds. When you use the basic building blocks of philanthropy toward a purpose, over time you can achieve a larger goal than you might imagine with any single gift.

### Give the Spending Rate or Give the Endowment, or Both— Then Repeat

Sylvia built her classic virtual endowment on the certain knowledge that she was going to make a significant bequest through her estate. But Sylvia was anything but a simple donor.

Many donors will put a toe in the water with their early gifts. Sylvia Initially was providing the "maintenance" spending rate, an annual gift that provided scholarship support for a single student. In her will, she had a commitment for the minimum amount that would ultimately be needed to endow that scholarship upon her demise.

Over the years, she was so satisfied with this program of giving that she duplicated it several times, such that her annual gifts have been covering the maintenance of several students. At the same time, she increased her bequest as well, to

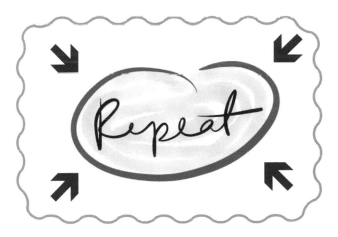

create full endowments for each of "her students," thus creating a scholars program of her own through combining both her lifetime and estate gifts.

There are many variations on this theme of creating multiple scholarships. Robert took a similar approach to creating, through his foundation, a program with multiple scholars. Rather than matching a bequest to each annual scholarship, as Sylvia did, he decided to create fully funded scholarships with each gift to create a much larger scholars program. How did this come about? His uncle had funded a single scholarship in memory of his father many years ago, and over the years some very impressive students had come through that program and become professors in their own right. Robert ultimately determined to make a long-term commitment from his foundation, such that each year's pledge payment would establish its own fully funded new scholarship in the name of his family.

## A Scholarship Financed with Annual Gifts and Balloon Payments

Doesn't know how to ask—Naive or sophisticated? To characterize as *naive* a person who is a sophisticated financial advisor and shrewd investor seems totally off base—until you learn the inside story. Harold and his wife Diane have a very deep and powerful charitable impulse. Yet, with all of his financial sophistication, it had never occurred to Harold that he might apply a key part of his financial knowledge to philanthropy.

However, once you have imagined an endowment program that is powered by a combination of current and future gifts (like a virtual endowment), you should have less difficulty imagining variations on this theme. Your problem-solving and collaboration can enable almost any donor with resources to make a meaningful charitable gift on their own terms, one that begins now and can be recognized immediately.

Harold and Diane have children who will soon graduate from college. They can envision a time not long in the future when the funds that have been going toward tuition might go for something else, perhaps something philanthropic.

Harold is a successful businessperson and investment manager. He understands how money can work in different ways and was willing to try applying some proven financing approaches to advance his own philanthropy. His plan enabled him to support a student in a novel way, consistent with his current and future prospects.

The funds for an outright scholarship will be coming on-stream when the children finish college. For the present, Harold and Diane are comfortable making annual gifts that could be used for the maintenance costs of a scholarship program (e.g., $7,500 each year for the first four years). Harold would equate this to a purchase or loan, just paying "interest" (really the annual maintenance) during the early years.

> ## How We Count It
>
> In this case, the financials would recognize a commitment to payments running over seven years ($7,500 x 7), including in the last three years balloon payments of $50,000. The total gift under the agreement would be $52,500 + $150,000 = $202,500.
>
>
> practical tip

Then, in the later years, while continuing to maintain the program with annual gifts, they would be able to make larger payments to build equity in their program and to fully establish their scholarship program ($7,500 + $50,000 for the last three years). In Harold's terms, from a financial perspective he would be making three balloon payments at the end of the term.

In any case, Harold and Diane were able to build a financial strategy that fit the terms of their lives. This meant their scholarship could begin immediately and that they would be recognized for the important support they were providing on a timely basis.

## Changing-up Your Own Game—For the Four (or More) Philanthropists in Your Life

As your comfort increases with the three game-changing killer apps, you can add great power to your gift-design practice. If you have a donor with resources and charitable intent, *and* you have the tools, you can work in a true alliance together, without the push-pull resistance and sales force dynamic that much fundraising seems to engender. The process becomes more donor driven: the objections and excuses that normally arise in the conventional (sometimes adversarial) solicitation of a gift are much less in evidence when you can site so many examples of how donors have achieved important goals on their own terms.

## Some Personalized Gift Designs
## Matched to Donors' Age, Needs, and Goals

| Donor Age | Personalized Gift Design | Gift Commitment | Type of Gift | Key Features |
|---|---|---|---|---|
| 80+/- | "Classic" virtual endowment. | Annual gift for life; expendable; maintains program.<br><br>Bequest for endowment secures the program for the future. | Two irrevocable pledges toward one program goal. | Program starts up right away; recognized; counted in campaign. |
| 65+/- | Testamentary pledge. | Bequest commitment.<br><br>Donors pledge portion of larger total gifts they have in mind and with which they are comfortable. | Irrevocable pledge. Not payable until death of donor; may be paid early. | Program cannot start up until donor's passing, but irrevocable gifts can be recognized immediately. |
| 50+/- | Equity-building philanthropic mortgage. | Annual gifts that are greater than the spending rate; excess of annual need goes to build endowment.<br><br>May include a down payment or a balloon payment at end of term. | Irrevocable pledge for a term of years; builds equity while program operates from start-up. | Program impact and recognition start now. Allows younger donor to benefit from modest-spending-rate gifts while they build legacy endowment over time. |

## Some Personalized Gift Designs
## Matched to Donors' Age, Needs, and Goals

| Donor Age | Personalized Gift Design | Gift Commitment | Type of Gift | Key Features |
|---|---|---|---|---|
| 40+/- | Limited virtual endowment. | Annual gift expendable for a certain number of years. | Irrevocable pledge. | Younger as older donor. Gifts of spending rate. Program "as if" endowed. |
| 40+/- | Hybrid bequest plus annual gifts. | Testamentary pledge for bequest; with revocable annual gifts. Irrevocable pledge of bequest. | Revocable annual gifts. | Program begins and operates as long as annual gifts; assured by bequest. |
| 40+/- | Hybrid annual gifts plus bequest. | Donor pledges to annual gifts for number of years; revocable intent for bequest. Irrevocable pledge of annual gifts. | Revocable bequest intent. | Program assured for a number of years; possible bequest. |

As the commentary states so well, as we all possess the Four Children within ourselves, perhaps we also possess the four donors: we are in essence speaking to the wise, wicked, simple, and unable-to-ask elements in all of us.

### The Passover Haggadah and Philanthropy

*Certainly there are obvious analogies between the ideals of the Haggadah and the ideals of philanthropy. Since the Four Sons is an all-inclusive trope: I'm in, I'm out, I haven't thought about that question, and I didn't know one could ask questions, there is a ready comparison that can be made to four types of donors who are seeking an education as to why to do philanthropy.*

*The Haggadah as well as philanthropy stresses the communal responsibility of all participants. Both remind us of the hazards of the world that require attention.*

*Both hope to take us from need to success and our right to celebrate that success.*

*Both remind us that the task is unending.*

Rabbi Steven Steinberg

## Thought Experiments for Donors

Would you give with a "warm hand" if you could? If you consider giving with a warm hand to mean not only giving while alive but also directing and designating the use of your future gifts, does that way of thinking open up the possibilities for you to give more or give differently? Do you believe that your legacy should be decided by someone else? If not you, who?

When one thinks of meeting donors "where they are," where would you think of yourself on the spectrum? In the range and capacity from wise (Astute), wicked (Questioning), simple (Curious), doesn't know how to ask (Searching), where are you? Are you always in the same place, or is there a variance from time to time? If you are giving away your treasure, what should you expect to gain from your gifts?

Do you expect a financial return, a spiritual redemption, or some other kind of ROI? What "impact" or change are you looking for? If you could, would you like to have more personal and interactive relationship with representatives of the organization or cause whose programs and projects will ultimately benefit from your support and generosity? Would you like to gain access to special people?

Do these personalized giving techniques help you see new ways to give? To investors and nonprofit administrators, endowment is a very specific management concept. But to you as a donor, it may mean simply ensuring that a goal will continue to be met long into the future. Which is most important to you, the investment or the use of the funds to achieve a goal? How do you set the balance?

Does it seem reasonable and possible to borrow familiar concepts from the rest of your life (say, the idea of a mortgage) and import them into philanthropy? Have you encountered charitable organizations that allow you to "build equity" in your endowment while also having it work at full capacity, as in these examples? Must you wait to "pay for your house before you live in it?" If not, are you willing and able to lead the way and show them how to have impact that begins right now? *Sometimes a donor goes from "one who does not know how to ask" to one who leads.*

Can you see how some of the basic building blocks of philanthropy—the seemingly modest outright gifts you make every year—could become the basis of a much more powerful gift later on? Have you thought about making a commitment (not just a pledge) over multiple years, instead of one year at a time, and what that could mean to an institution you care about?

If you decided to lead with your annual gifts (and turn a traditional endowment on its head), how could your ultimate gift have even greater impact than if you used those modest gifts to grow an endowment?

Using personalized philanthropy, how might you suggest new ways to reconfigure your own approaches to giving to achieve greater impact and recognition, starting now?

## To Recap

◆ Meeting donors "where they are" involves understanding their comfort level with giving away their treasure and what they want or expect to gain from their gifts.

◆ Endowment is a very specific investment concept to nonprofit administrators, but to donors, it simply means ensuring that a goal will continue to be met long into the future. In personalized philanthropy, the focus is on the goal, not on the investment concept.

◆ Start with concepts—like the mortgage—that are familiar to donors and engage them in applying those concepts to philanthropy in creative ways to meet their goals.

# Chapter Four

## Moving Beyond Conventional Solicitation: New Best Practices for Personalized Philanthropy

### IN THIS CHAPTER

- ···→ What is the value of a disorderly mind?

- ···→ What are best practices you could apply toward the new discipline of personalized philanthropy?

- ···→ How to build powerful guiding teams—from having the whole system in one room to ad hoc mini-design teams

- ···→ Three sample elements in a personalized gift agreement (virtual Endowment)

This chapter is a discussion about the process of personalized gift design and how it differs from conventional gift solicitation. I want to explore what really happens when a gift officer sits down to have a conversation with a donor about philanthropy.

As I have noted, I am a regular commuter between the two cultures of fundraising—the synthetic institution-focused and the more organic donor-focused world of personalized philanthropy. I'd like to describe how the solicitation process appears from each perspective. You may recognize yourself in one or even both of these worlds. Here's a spoiler alert: for me, the best approach to donor solicitation boils down to cultivating a

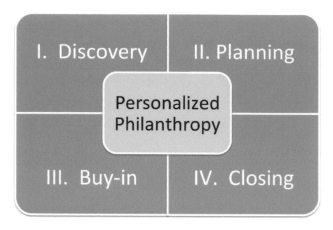

somewhat disorderly but very well-prepared mind, where the full spectrum of philanthropic solutions is on the table. I know full well that this is not how it is usually done.

When I reflect about the gifts that are illustrated in this book, as well as the ones that I am working on with colleagues right now, I see a few commonalities in the way they come about. Rather than strictly *prescribing* steps to be followed, it is more that I am *observing* four steps or phases that seem to naturally emerge from a process of dynamic interactions with donors and stakeholders:

1. Discovery

2. Planning

3. Buy-in

4. Closing

## Best Practice #1: Discovery

Discovery is envisioning. For me, this is always the first and most important best practice. The good things that can happen if you just "let it be" are often the things left out when there is a rush to judgment.

Driven by curiosity and passion shared by both the donor and the gift officer, discovery is the first essential step in meeting the challenge to mesh the dual interests of donor and institution. We want to learn whatever we can about what is important to the donor and what drives and motivates decisions and actions and emotions.

There are so many different formulations of discovery-type questions that have been posed by so many development experts. But I am most interested in the principles behind these questions: homework before the interview, honest curiosity, empathy, active listening, and reflection when the interview is done.

### *Zen and the Art of Gift Planning*

"One of the advantages of being disorderly is that one is constantly making exciting discoveries."

—Alan Alexander Milne (1882–1956)

"Did you ever observe to whom the accidents happen? Chance favors only the prepared mind."

—Louis Pasteur (1822–1895)

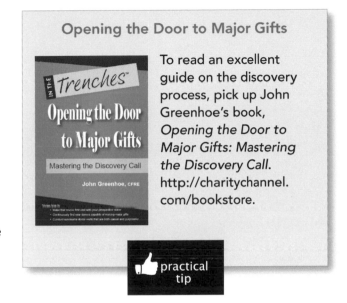

**Opening the Door to Major Gifts**

To read an excellent guide on the discovery process, pick up John Greenhoe's book, *Opening the Door to Major Gifts: Mastering the Discovery Call.* http://charitychannel. com/bookstore.

practical tip

"Those are my principles. If you don't like them I have others."

—Groucho Marx (1890-1977)

A word about these quotes, including Groucho's: I am not admitting to having no moral compass! Instead, it's a reminder that when interviewing a donor, the approach that works best for me is to have no preconceived notion of what I will do after the conversation. It is true, however, that putting aside notions of the conventional solicitation process can seem like inviting chaos into the room. While embracing the disorderly is definitely a risk, the payoff is a gift of authenticity—both to the donor and from the donor to you. I mean, if I am a planned gift officer bound to operate within the fundraising Matrix and I am there to "sell" a gift annuity, eventually it will all come down to that. Won't it?

The challenge of discovery, for me, is to adopt, and believe in, the style that has been called discernment: to listen with an open mind or even to cultivate an empty mind. I am not a question machine and my questions are not preplanned. Ironically, I will often work up a practice script, but this is not so much to consider what I will say as it is to discover what I think. I would not think of beginning with the same question twice. I don't want to drive the conversation to a specific point. Instead, you might try to channel your inner Terry Gross or Barbara Walters, or think of some guiding spirit that flies free. Mine is over there—a crow or raven on one of the peaks at Zion national park.

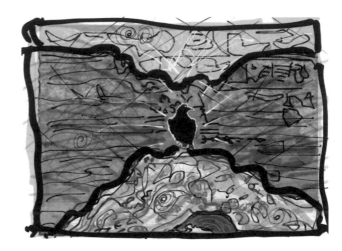

## Negative Capability

The interview with a donor is more a watchful waiting than a waiting to pounce. What is important is your capability to be an active listener, but at the same time, not too active. Perhaps the poet, John Keats, put it best when he spoke of embracing uncertainty: "I mean negative capability, that is, when a man is capable of being in uncertainties, mysteries, doubts, without any irritable reaching after fact and reason . . . ." You might want to give it a try.

## A Success Story

A close colleague, Eden Graber, asked me to join her for a meeting with a prospect, Alex, she had been cultivating for some time. Introduced to her by a financial advisor, she knew Alex both had the means and the desire to fund something important in Alzheimer's disease. Over the course of a year, she had met and gotten to know him and had suggested a variety of gifts. Each time he responded positively but would not act. She felt she had missed something, something key to activating him to move toward finalizing a gift. She asked me to join her to be a second, discerning, listener.

She had given me a thorough briefing but, on the spur of the moment, a few minutes before we met face-to-face I looked him up online. What struck me was that the first several entries were all about a professorial chair he had established in his mother's name. She had suffered with Alzheimer's for a long time before her death. While there were many other details about him, these first entries stayed with me.

At Alex's request, we met for breakfast in a small, harshly lit diner located near his (two!) Central Park West apartments, refusing anything fancier. He turned out to be quirky and fun and very serious at the same time. While I hesitated to ask him a deeply personal question on our first meeting, my curiosity prodded me forward and I did ask why, of all the things he could have done, had it been so important to him that his first major journey into philanthropy was to create a memorial for his mother? His response was thoughtful and detailed, and revealed a desire that his gift be recognized in the United States, where his mother had lived. As we left the meeting, he turned to my colleague and said, "In the words of Winston Churchill, 'never, never, never give up.'"

She didn't. She wrote him a deeply personal letter that contained another proposal for a different type of gift, one based on what we had heard that morning. No response. It was a full year later, when Alex himself passed away, before we learned the impact of having had that conversation and the follow-up letter. Alex had felt heard, and had come to envision *for the first time* what he wanted to achieve with his philanthropy. Without informing us, he had adopted virtually all of our proposed language into his living trust, making a gift to us that assured his specific wishes would be realized. This ultimate gift must have been very satisfying because he truly had understood what was most important to him.

Here are a few excerpts from the gift officer's extraordinary letter to the donor:

> *"Never, never, never give up." That's what you said, quoting Winston Churchill, and I took you at your word—hence, this letter and a brief proposal.*

> *I felt our conversation, just before I left for Israel, was an honest and real meeting of the minds and a breakthrough of sorts. Thank you for speaking plainly about the importance of having you and your mother's legacy live on in the United States.*

> *I wish I had realized sooner how important it is to show you that the Institute's research on Alzheimer's disease is not just about what happens*

*in Israel but reaches and involves and is recognized by people all over the world. Science today is global, collaborative, and reaches beyond borders to draw in the best minds.*

*Alex, we can designate that your gift to the Institute is used to support this, to support collaborative research, preferably in the United States, and that all the ingredients for your legacy in the United States through support of the Institute in Israel are present.*

*A perfect example of how this could work occurred to me just last week, in Israel, when I attended the first, named international annual scientific conference for a cancer donor. I was privileged to be there with the donor. It was quite special, for I had, with him, worked to actually shape the gift that resulted in our sitting together in Israel in a conference room filled with stellar scientists and physicians from leading institutions in the United States, Israel, Great Britain—the world. They were all actively working together to advance treatment through basic research that informed translational approaches.*

*As our own meeting was still fresh in my mind, I imagined what it would be like to sit with you in a similar room, watching top scientists from around the world coming together to try to find preventions, treatment, or a cure for Alzheimer's disease.*

*Your Fund for Alzheimer's and Neuroscience Research could make this type of annual gathering in your name possible. While the funding would come from your trust on your demise, you have the opportunity now, while you are alive, to direct the use of your funds in a way that is meaningful to you.*

*Here is sample language that your trustee might include in your trust to establish The _____Fund for Alzheimer's and Neuroscience Research... .*

*I sincerely hope that we have fully appreciated what is most meaningful to you to achieve with your philanthropy and captured your intent in this proposal... .*

For me, the questions can all be reduced to a search for meaning, connection, and relationship between the donor and the institution. I want to help the donor arrive at a gift that provides the greatest possible support for the mission, with impact, and recognition that can begin immediately. That is clearly my own personal motivation and bias toward action, and I am unashamed to share my aims with any donor who wants to know what my agenda is. The renaming of my department not long ago from the institution-focused "Planned Giving" to the donor-focused "Center for Personalized Philanthropy" provides me the opportunity to express this often.

## Personalized Donor Profiling in 360 degrees

There are so many dimensions to the discovery process. My own approach is based on the concept of a 360-degree donor-focused model. This is helpful for assessing a donor before acting, as well as for putting together the right kind of team, if one is needed.

In my previous position, I had global responsibility for managing donor relationships. Now I am more narrowly focused on problem solving and gift designing solutions for individual donors. I often work with other gift officers. I become engaged with our staff when I refer a donor who responded to our gift marketing to a colleague, or when I am called in by a colleague who wants to consider these gift designs I've called killer apps with one of her own prospects. The two of us can operate as a "mini-design team" in considering what course to take with the donor.

Whoever I am working with, I want both to share and to learn everything I can about the donor. I think I have an inquiring mind, and my personal bias towards action does not allow me to "rest in research" for too long or to be paralyzed by too much information. Sometimes, like most major gift people, I want to jump ahead almost too quickly, so I invoke the discovery process as a way to think first and avoid jumping toward action too soon.

Moves Management theory, as practiced by William Sturtevant, suggests bringing the donor into contact with "natural peer partners," lay leaders, peers, and friends who are already well-connected with the organization. I try to adapt that approach whenever possible to personalized philanthropy.

Extending this idea, there can also be a natural staff partner that will work best with a given donor, and the truth is, I'd like to be that person in most cases. Going even further, there can be a program person, like a scientist or researcher or even a young student, who will also connect best with a particular donor. Finding out who these people are can make all the difference. If someone else in your system has already identified natural partners, you'd like to know about it. So your discovery is not only with the donor, it is with the people on staff and elsewhere who know the donor best.

This model of interdisciplinary or multidisciplinary staffing of a donor in 360 degrees helps assure a higher level of connection and stewardship, tying together what happens in every sphere of our interaction, from events to gift conversations, so the donor's experience of us is truly seamless. On a good day, we are very good at this cross-boundary, collaborative, and multidisciplinary approach to gift planning.

### Design Team Acquires New Donor

I recently helped assemble a team to help with acquisition of a new donor who responded to direct mail. She was interested in exploring a bequest. Before calling her, I looked into her giving history. It was very sparse, but I noticed her neighborhood was right on the Florida beachfront. I called my colleague in that region and he said, "Good address." He looked into history, while I contacted her and arranged a visit in response to her inquiry.

My colleague discovered that our donor had, in fact, attended one of his events where a scientist spoke about a topic of great interest to her. My colleague and I met with her together, and then he arranged several sessions at her home with visiting professors who talked about scholarships, in which she was very interested. We provided language she could use to place our organization in her will to support young students, but we also suggested ways to begin making a difference sooner than upon her demise.

She decided pretty much without prompting that she did not need a charitable gift annuity or the income it could provide. Instead, she made a pledge so we had assurance of receiving at the least a small part of the gift she had planned in her estate. We were able to recognize this commitment with a substantial naming opportunity of a student auditorium. In the future, she may decide to make additional gifts so she can see students benefit from her scholarship support during her lifetime. This donor connected with us in a variety of ways, through a number of people. Her initial experience with one of our scientists inspired her to respond to me. Other staff, scientists and administrators became engaged and we all connected in a very satisfying and seamless manner.

stories from the real world

I have spent a great deal of time trying to understand the donor in the big picture of our organization, without regard to different fundraising silos. In order to do that, I built a nonlinear mind map to try to capture all of it.

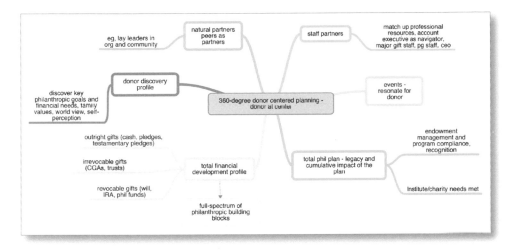

The map, of course, is not a map, but a "discovery profile" of everything we need to learn or consider about a donor and the donor's values. Who are the donor's natural peer and staff partners? What special events resonated? What previous gifts has the donor made? Why, how, and with what assets? With those previous gifts, how were compliance and commitments fulfilled? What kind of program or project would engage the donor? Where does the donor fit in the social system of our organization? All of it!

Clearly, many people will see this as a perfect example of TMI—too much information! But if you use or even internalize something like this 360-degree donor-focused profile, you can get a real handle on what is going on with a donor. If you and your colleagues are going to try to meet donors "where they are," especially if they are very important prospects for you, you owe it to yourself to look a little deeper and find the sweet spot where your donor and your organization can connect most strongly. When it really counts, this is not one of those times for the ready, fire, aim approach, where you want to just get out there and ask. In cases where you need to prepare, this can really help.

## Between Now and Then—Closing with *That* Donor

Another Discovery trick I play on myself—and sometimes I drag a close colleague into it with me—is to imagine a particularly important donor, one whose gift really made our campaign that year. We know what this donor has already done—now we try to predict where the donor will go next. How could the donor get to the place to finally make the gift of our dreams? (Notice I said "our" dreams, but no gift will be made if it doesn't capture the donor's dream as well.)

For example, we may see that one thing standing between the donor and a dream gift is the sale of a business. I have time to think about what I could do to help with the donor exit strategy. I might make an introduction to a mergers/acquisitions person who is a friend, or even another donor. I'm a match-maker in the best sense, helping our donors without being intrusive. In the same way, you can imagine who a donor (like our beachfront prospect) might meet to inspire a new level of commitment, or what naming opportunity would be particularly meaningful.

If you are in collaboration with close colleagues across the organization, then you can make the things happen that are necessary for donors to have those breakthrough conversations and relationships that can inspire truly transformational gifts. But keep in mind that to acquire a transformational gift, you need to be ready to be transformed as well.

### Discovery Is Envisioning

Looking at both your donor and your organization in 360 degrees, doing your own version of curiosity-driven research aimed at first identifying, and later meshing and shaping into a workable gift agreement, the donor's compelling interests with your organization's most compelling needs. Without vision there can be no gift.

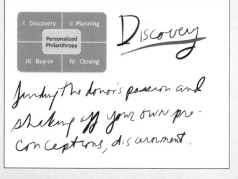

## Best Practice #2: Planning

If discovery is about envisioning, then planning is about shaping. It's a highly interactive phase between the gift officer and the donor. All gift arrangements and vehicles—the full spectrum of philanthropic building blocks—are on the table. At the same, all of the institution's needs and priorities are also on the table. After discovery, planning is the process of seeing what sticks, and shaping new forms for gifts and seeing what forms of giving will match up with what kinds of programs.

This is the stage where gifts mentioned in other chapters took their shape. We test a gift structure against the kinds of program impacts the donor would like to have to see if it will achieve what is intended. For example, remember the donor who was burdened with high expenses now from kids in college, with cash flow expected to improve later? Or the donor who is building a real estate business today, and who foresees a revenue event in a few years? If these donors are eager to make a substantial impact on your mission, they will not be able to make a substantial outright gift today to fully fund a program. But, they may be able to make more modest annual gifts of the "spending rate" that will cover the annual program costs for the next several years. This gift may come from a current income stream, or it might be the product of a charitable gift annuity, if they are old enough to have one.

The "right gift, for the right donor" might turn out to be a commitment to several years of annual gifts, with a progressively larger payment toward the end of a five-year term. Even a balloon payment at the end of the term could be considered.

### *Shaping Long-Term Gifts*

Gift-shaping and, eventually, closing are different in donor-focused personalized philanthropy than in institution-focused fundraising. Especially with the killer apps, the terms can be much more flexible, enabling both the donor and the institution to, well, get more done. Essentially, these gift apps reapply basic and familiar financial transactions to the sphere of philanthropy.

Consider that most organizations will only consider a term of three to five years for a pledge, cash payments are usually required, and the programs cannot begin until they are fully funded. Given these restrictions, many fundraisers will have to walk away from a donor who has been giving for many years in the past, and has a gift in a will, because there is no structural way to meet this donor's goal for significant impact.

In the new shaping process, the objective is to satisfy the desire for impact and recognition *now*. For the donor mentioned above, a legally binding pledge can be structured as a "philanthropic mortgage" and build equity while it runs five to ten years, with a down-payment now or a balloon at the end, or a gradually increasing payment. Whatever will work for both donor and institution, within reason and law and the bounds of good sense, can be considered.

Through the discovery and shaping process, the donor is actively engaged with you in reality-testing alternative ways of achieving the donor's goal, continuously refining and reflecting as you go. I've said you are only limited by your imagination in many of these cases—assuming, of course, that you are not limited in your explorations by your gift acceptance policies or organizational silos! The goal is to design a custom gift app for a particular donor, based on the donor's particular set of facts, while never losing sight of what is most important to your organization.

The tools you have at your disposal are every building block of philanthropy. Outright gifts, irrevocable charitable remainder and lead trusts and charitable gift annuities, revocable bequest "intentions," and much more. The personalized gift apps enable you to use these building blocks in the best way to achieve your shared goal with the donor of impact upon your organization and its mission.

### Design Team Input

During the planning phase, sometimes it's a good idea to bring together what we'd call a design team to help determine a course of action. This is a concept we've implemented for top donors and special kinds of prospects, but you can use it for all donors, all the time.

Design team members are drawn from the staffing previously referred to in the 360 degree view of the donor. They include people who know and work best with the donor, as well as executives of the organization who can make the tough decisions, and people who are good with strategy. Theoretically, when the right people are on the team, you should be able to move organizational mountains or cut bureaucratic red tape that gift officers acting alone would not be able to manage by themselves. This is a small but mighty group with knowledge and decision-making authority— by definition: a powerful guiding team. They are empowered to make the things happen that need to happen.

## Guiding Team Overkill

Some years ago at a staff retreat, we brought together the most powerful guiding team that could be imagined. This was to be a demonstration project on the effectiveness of design teams and the 360-degree approach.

The design team for this exercise consisted of the chief executives from *both* the fundraising and program sides of the organization. We had assembled "the whole system" in one room in order to gain a profound understanding of one donor. As in basic science, we followed curiosity and passion for discovery, with no idea where they would end. The rest of the staff attending the conference observed the group's dynamic. With essentially our whole world watching, we demonstrated design teams and how the 360-degree approach could work at the highest level.

After that, it was up to us to implement them, or not, in our own world and at a scale that would be most practical and cost-effective. The opportunity for the two sides of the gift equation, donor-focus and institution-focus, to come together? Priceless.

Since then, both formal and informal mini-design teams have been convened on many occasions. One team guided a mini-campaign to identify and engage the organization's top volunteer leadership. Another has been part of an initiative to increase support from structured foundations, particularly those going into second and third generations. Informal, ad hoc, or mini-design teams have become a common practice between gift planning staff managers.

## Best Practice #3: Buy-in

Buy-in is about structuring. It is the essential move from verbal to written, from the improvised and free form to purposeful and deliberate, where understandings that will soon go into a gift agreement are crafted and shaped. This is where the final structure of the gift is explained and disclosed, often in a formal proposal or vision document or prospectus. At

## Planning Is Shaping

It builds on information from discovery to shape gift designs and make recommendations. This is accomplished by providing the illustrations and proposals you have learned would be of greatest interest to the donor. It is a free-form trial period of reality testing options for meshing the donor's compelling interests and your organization's compelling needs.

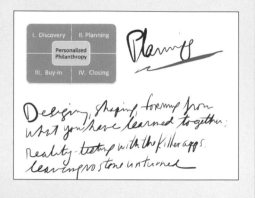

the same time, it's an invitation to close the gift, from each side to the other. Do we have it right yet? Before closing, you must have buy-in.

There is so much you can say about this phase. If you don't have it, you can derail the entire gift process and have no closing. This is where you get it right or wrong, because as a gift officer, this is where you commit it all to paper. Are your recommendation and the culmination of your "shared" understanding with the donor really shared?

### Where Quality Control Happens

Buy-in is for all the stakeholders, both on the side of the donor and on the side of the institution. Don't make promises that others can't keep. At this point, negotiations with the donor and the donor's team have either been concluded, or new issues will surface.

This moment is for obtaining full understanding, engagement, participation, and commitment to a specific recommendation for a gift and financial plan. To be successful, all the stakeholders need to have been identified, considered, and brought in to the particulars of the plan, including the tax and legal implications, the expressions of charitable intent of the donor, and any other legal or ethical considerations. Quality control at this point ensures that promises made both by the donor and your organization can be met; the terms of the gift are clarified; and the shared vision and intentions of the gift are made explicit.

### Where Buy-in Can Go Wrong ... or Right

Most of the stories about buy-in are about when it goes wrong and the pledge is never signed. But glitches can also be opportunities. Consider a donor who has remembered your organization in a will and wants to establish a special fund. If you have built your plan around the donor making an irrevocable commitment to a bequest on her death, and she is not comfortable with that, your gift can go wrong. However, if you have built your plan around a revocable letter of intent rather than a binding pledge—and, by *binding* pledge, I mean one that is supported by consideration—you will have a much better chance of completing a gift. In this case, you would have a gift agreement or a letter of intent with a revocable commitment, rather than a pledge agreement.

In one case, I worked with a donor who would not sign a pledge, but was very willing to establish a number of charitable gift annuities during his lifetime as an expression of the seriousness of his charitable intent. This donor wanted to create a memorial fund for his partner, who had very close ties with founders of our organization. We arranged for the proceeds of the gift annuities to be added to the bequest we ultimately received. When the donor passed away, his bequest was large and much greater than the three gift annuities that had been established during life. The memorial fund was then established with the bequest and the remaining proceeds from the gift annuities.

> ### I Promise That's a Pledge
>
> A pledge is a promise to make a charitable contribution in the future. As with any promise, it could be nonbinding or binding. To be binding, it must be supported by consideration. Though this topic is beyond the scope of this book, just know that, when I refer to a pledge, I am speaking of a binding pledge that is fully enforceable.
>
>  definition

In a similar case, where the donor would not sign a pledge, she had assigned several bank accounts for transfer on her death. After the terrorist attacks on 9/11, having saved more than a million dollars during her lifetime, she decided she wanted to make a gift she found especially life-affirming. She now makes a gift every year from her IRA, especially during the years when retirement gifts can be contributed as charitable rollovers. Her gift agreement gives her assurance that her bequest ultimately will be used for creating the special fund she has in mind.

In a completely different case, the donor, a teacher, could not buy in to the plan he, himself, had helped develop. He had agreed to a testamentary pledge to establish a program. Because the commitment was irrevocable and binding, and there was even some public recognition that would be granted, the donor mistakenly thought that the program could begin immediately. He was very disappointed to learn that was not the case. However, he had been making regular annual gifts for years that were close to the annual costs of the program, so he decided to slightly stretch his annual gift and make an additional pledge commitment. In addition to the bequest commitment, he would agree to maintain the program's annual costs for five years, minimum. Under this new agreement, his program would now be able to start immediately, based on his annual gifts. Most important, an incumbent would be named immediately. He would still have the assurance of his program becoming fully funded through his bequest, so that it would continue in the years to come. That was an agreement worthy of his buy-in.

There are just some times when a donor will not want to sign that pledge. You can review the two alternatives: a non-legally-binding gift agreement based on the donor's wishes, hopes, plans, and dreams versus a gift agreement which is designed to be

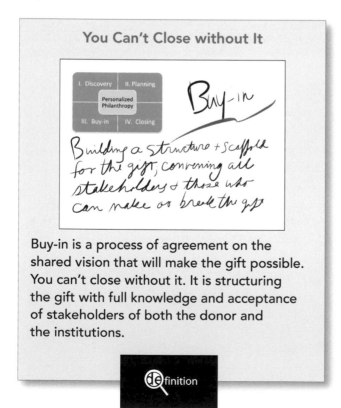

## You Can't Close without It

Buy-in

Building a structure + scaffold for the gift, convening all stakeholders + those who can make or break the gift

Buy-in is a process of agreement on the shared vision that will make the gift possible. You can't close without it. It is structuring the gift with full knowledge and acceptance of stakeholders of both the donor and the institutions.

definition

legally binding and enforceable on both the parties. Then, the aim in the conversations with the donor is to clarify the difference and sharpen the distinctions. Ambiguity generally does not make for a good plan and is, frankly, poor practice.

## Best Practice #4: Closing

If discovery is the opening, documenting a gift agreement for the record is the closing. But it's more. Closing is anchoring the gift, both in the law and in the heart.

Words matter. I am not an attorney, so when I think about gift agreements, my perspective is different than those who study contracts and the parsing of words for legal purposes. Over my career, I've been very fortunate to work closely with attorneys, in-house and general counsel who share charitable aims and values, and who think clearly and shoot straight. Without involvement of trained and committed legal professionals, it would not have been possible to translate these ideas about donor-focused philanthropy into gift arrangements suited to the needs and interests of so many donors, as well as our organization.

That being said, while the task of the closing is primarily to achieve clarity for legal purposes, secondarily it is critical to achieve clarity for both the donor and the institution that will need to carry the programs forward and implement them.

The legal hurdles of closing generally cover the mutual commitments of the charity and the donor. They delineate clearly who the donor is, and take into account multiple signers and different kinds of legal entities who enter into the agreement. They cover payment schedules, naming and recognition, gift acceptance policies, and, of course, much more.

My focus naturally gravitates toward areas where the legal and the personal might be thought to overlap—to language and to wedge issues. I want to direct my comments mostly to these secondary, but still critical, matters. Here are just a few examples:

### Compliance and Fulfillment

Compliance in a *legal* sense is about following the terms of the agreement and keeping the promises you make: sending reports on time and maintaining good stewardship of the donor and being in compliance with legal standards and practices. But in another more personal sense, for the donor compliance is about gift fulfillment and achieving an impact. Institution-focused fundraising is generally about *getting* the gift, while donor-focused fundraising is about *keeping* the gift. We want the donor to stay engaged over the long term, especially since many of the gift designs include testamentary giving.

### Clarity of the Donor's Overall Vision

When I'm working with my legally-inclined colleague on a gift agreement, we hardly ever come to blows. In a gift agreement, there is a way for expressing legally binding language for a pledge and there's also a place for expressing the overall intent and vision of the donor. Most of our pledges include a section called "recitals" for these nonlegal aspects. The recitals section is the perfect place to let the donor's story shine through. It is essential that the donor is reflected in the agreement. That vision of this gift is something the donor has worked hard to achieve, and if the gift is made in honor or in memory of a significant person or if the donor is "giving back" or making the gift for a cause, this should be recorded as well as the legal aspects. In a sense, many donors look to their gift agreements to become an "ethical will." They take heart to see some expression of their human and family values come through, despite the legalese in other parts of the document. I think they know best.

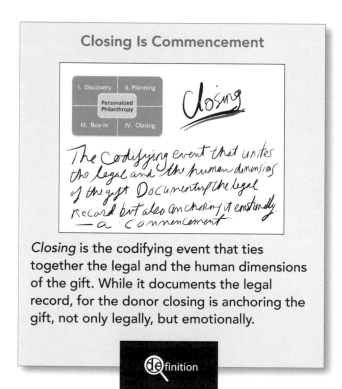

**Closing Is Commencement**

The codifying event that unites the legal and the human dimensions of the gift. Documenting the legal record but also anchoring it emotionally. — a "Commencement"

*Closing* is the codifying event that ties together the legal and the human dimensions of the gift. While it documents the legal record, for the donor closing is anchoring the gift, not only legally, but emotionally.

**definition**

### Clear Delineation of Irrevocable and Revocable Elements

Many gift agreements include both a pledge and a statement of donative intent. Consider two contrasting examples:

◆ In one gift design, the donor wanted to make a pledge for annual gifts towards scholarship funds for five years, and expressed her intent to endow the scholarship on her death with a bequest in her will. She had already executed the bequest in the will, but she was not willing or ready at that time to make a legal commitment to a specific gift amount.

◆ In another gift design, the donor wanted to make a legally binding pledge for a bequest from his estate that would fund scholarships. But at the same time, he expressed his hope and intent to make annual gifts of a certain minimum amount so the program may be started up in his lifetime. He had been making annual gifts on a regular basis for many years, but for his own reason, he did not want to be bound by continuing to do so.

## A Process for Moving Beyond Convention

As I think back, there are so many stories about gift officers (and I'll include myself as a novice among them) wanting to bring proposals and even blank gift agreements to their early meetings with donors.

*Maybe that donor will, in fact, want to go forward with a charitable gift annuity right away!*

*Maybe the donor will have a check in hand for us!*

*Maybe the donor will tell us after all this time that our organization is in the will and here's a little down payment on the bequest!*

*We could accept that gift and return to the office and everyone would be pleased and praise our outstanding fundraising ability!*

More than likely, no one would give a second thought to what might have been or what might yet be. If there is any point in following the four steps I've outlined to move from opening to closing a gift, it is to learn this: There is value in recognizing the thoughtful, intentional and even organic process that naturally accompanies success in gift solicitation. And there are also moments where a disorderly but prepared mind may be the only thing that gets you through.

Having followed, or perhaps having been swept along through, this four-step approach, I think you will often find that for both donor and gift officer, the signing of a gift agreement is very much like a graduation ceremony: less a closing than a commencement.

## Three Sample Elements in a Personalized Gift Agreement (Virtual Endowment)

Here are examples of the component parts described throughout this process. I hope it is obvious that they are not intended for use in your agreements but simply to clarify the steps along the way, as might artifacts or your notes of conversations about is important to you and your donors.

### Recitals

Recitals are not part of the pledge or legally binding aspect, but they can serve to personalize the arrangement for a donor, future gift office staff, those engaged in compliance, and family members who want to understand what their relative had in mind by making the gift.

---

**Example of Recitals in a Charitable Pledge**

Whereas, Donor wishes to follow philanthropically in the footsteps of her father (of blessed memory) who ardently supported _____ through many years of annual gifts;

Whereas, Donor has already included _____ in her estate plan and served as co-chair of a women's mission and wishes to provide an example of leadership, which may be emulated by other participants;

Whereas, donor has already contributed $250,000 towards an intended giving-circle commitment of $1 million;

Whereas, for these reasons and Donor's own passion for curiosity, discovery, and imagination, Donor has now decided to commit to pledging a portion of the total gift she has envisioned, payable at or by the time of her passing, to provide perpetual support for curiosity-driven research;

Whereas, in consideration of and reliance upon this new pledge, _____ has agreed to establish [Family Name] Discovery Fund.

**Example**

### *Testamentary Pledge*

A testamentary pledge is like any other pledge, except that it is understood to be payable on the demise of the donor. In many cases, unlike other pledges, there may not be a specific payment schedule because the expectation is that the payment will come from the estate of the donor. These pledges may, however, be satisfied in a number of ways, including during the lifetime of the donor.

We usually specify if the pledge is to be paid upon the death of the donor, or if it may be reduced by gifts made during lifetime. This is especially important if the pledge payable on death is intended to endow a program, which the donor is supporting with annual or other lifetime gifts through a virtual endowment.

If this is not made clear, the donor's executor may rightfully claim that a portion of the pledge has been satisfied during the donor's lifetime, and therefore there may be less principal available to create an endowment that will be needed to perpetuate the annual spending for the program.

### *Start-up Agreement for a Virtual Endowment*

A virtual endowment is the classic flexible endowment that combines a series of annual gifts that pay for the maintenance of a program or project, and a balloon or ultimate gift payment that is intended to endow or perpetuate the program. The annual payment can be the spending rate on an endowment, while the balloon payment could correspond to the corpus or principal of an endowment or a legacy fund.

The start-up agreement can be included along with the testamentary pledge, or separated. In this case, I've shown it as a separate agreement or add-on. Both aspects could be included in a single unified agreement, which would be like an umbrella that covered all aspects of a long-term agreement.

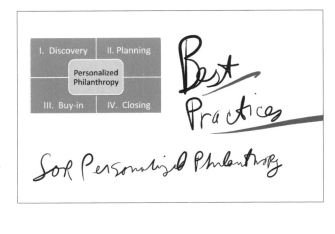

### Example of a Testamentary Pledge

Now, therefore, in consideration of the mutual obligations and covenants set forth herein, the parties agree as follows:

1. Pledge
   a. Donor hereby pledges to make a minimum new gift of $1 million ("Legacy Pledge").
   b. Donor intends for the Legacy Pledge to be paid via her estate or a combination of the following:
      1) A bequest in Donor's will or living trust.
      2) Gift or gifts of cash, marketable securities, or other property that is acceptable.
      3) A percentage designation from an IRA or a qualified pension plan.
      4) Death benefits of a life insurance policy.
      5) Other means acceptable and in keeping with the Internal Revenue Code and relevant state and federal law.
   c. Donor covenants that she shall be liable for payment of the pledge and the balance shall be paid as an obligation of her estate.

2. Use of Monies, Establishment of Fund

   As recognition, consideration, and reliance on Donor's pledges herein, _____ shall establish [The Donor's] Discovery Fund for Women in Science. Charity retains control over the Fund, and acknowledges preference for support of women scientists.

3. Recognition and Naming
   a. To honor Donor in the President's Circle, recognizing donors who have given $1 million or more.
   b. To provide Donor or designated representatives with periodic updates.
   c. To ensure appropriate recognition on the Donor Wall.
   d. To induct Donor into the Honor Society, recognizing those who have included _____ in their estate plans.
   e. To acknowledge the source of funding in publications or professional journals (whenever possible).
   f. To plan future expenditures based on the expectation of the fulfillment of the pledges herein.

_____       _____
            Donor                                    Date

_____       _____
     Executive Vice President                         Date

**Example**

These samples should not be taken as advice about how to construct legally binding agreements, but as examples of how personalized gift designs can be structured. For example, it is also possible to structure a gift that grows from a master's scholarship to a doctoral scholarship, or even a professorial chair, either during life or after death. Flexibility is the key to personalizing gift agreements.

---

### Example of a Start-up Pledge

Whereas, Donor has pledged to provide, by the time of her passing, funds for the Donor Discovery Fund;

Whereas, Donor would now like to initiate such fund with annual payments for ten years;

Whereas, in consideration and reliance upon this additional gift, _____ shall immediately name the fund _____;

Now, therefore, the parties agree as follows:

1. Annual Pledge. Donor pledges to make a gift of $150,000, according to the following payment schedule: $15,000 payable for each of ten years, commencing on or before June 30, 20____.

   Donor covenants that she shall be liable for payment of the balance of this annual pledge, and that the balance of this annual pledge remaining upon her death shall be paid as an obligation of such estate.

2. Allocation of Payments/Naming of Discovery Fund. _____ agrees that the proceeds of each payment of this annual pledge shall be used to provide immediate, expendable support for basic science research with the donor's preference for women scientists.

3. _____ agrees to provide other recognition to Donor commensurate with this additional level of giving.

_____        _____
              Donor                                          Date

_____        _____
       Executive Vice President                            Date

**Example**

## To Recap

◆ *Discovery* is more than anything else about following your curiosity and finding the donor's passion—shaking off preconceptions about what the donor wants as well as what you want. It's about being discerning, rather than deciding in advance what will be needed.

◆ *Planning* is envisioning, shaping, and forming a gift from what you and the donor have gleaned from your explorations, and reality-testing differing perspectives, leaving no stone unturned.

◆ *Buy-in* is building a structure and a scaffolding for the gift, being sure to include or recognize all those who can help make or break the gift. It is engaging your stakeholders.

◆ *Closing* is the codifying event that ties together the legal and the human dimensions of the gift. While as a representative of the institution you may be documenting the gift for the legal record, your donor is celebrating the beginning of a realization of the donor's greater philanthropic vision. For the donor, closing is anchoring the gift, not only legally, but emotionally.

# Chapter Five

## Counting, Numbers, Value, and the Big Picture

### IN THIS CHAPTER

- ···➔ How policies for counting gifts support personalized philanthropy.

- ···➔ Explain how planned gifts fit in the big picture of your fundraising program.

- ···➔ Defining yourself in terms of fundraising achievement, not solely in terms of financial results.

Curiously, all this donor-focused personalized gift planning began with a deceptively simple question: "How can I talk about numbers to the people who count?" Those people are not just the executives and chief financial officers who report audited financial results, but all of the stakeholders who should be "in the know," not just about the financials, but about *all* the numbers that shape our fundraising results.

Why do I say that this is curious? Because, if you are a fundraiser, you don't have to answer the question, "How much did you raise?" Someone else will always be ready to answer it for you. Chances are, even today, the answer will always be one-dimensional: One Number, derived from a financial formula (like the charitable deduction value prescribed by the IRS, or the discounted present value). There is no better evidence of the existence of a fundraising Matrix (or Matrix-like culture) than the almost universal requirement for gift reporting based solely on One Number.

I worked in the field as a planned giving officer for nearly ten years before I felt compelled to start writing and speaking about this vexing problem of how to *account* for what fundraisers do and how we *count* what we do.

My first insight years ago was that, except for some narrow purposes, you can't just count planned gifts. You have to have a way to understand the big picture of fundraising first and see where the planned as well as other types of gifts fit in. This will always be a multidimensional
task. Financial statements aside, fundraisers want our counting and reporting simply and transparently to reflect the way people actually structure their gifts, as outright, revocable, irrevocable, or a combination.

## Top Ten Signs That You're Ready to Shift

These are some of the vexing situations that led me to think about how we count gifts, which ultimately shapes how we create gifts. If you recognize yourself in these scenarios, it may be time for you to recommend a new approach:

1. Your audience that is most comfortable with numbers—e.g., nonprofit CFOs as well as some CEOs—turns out to have only limited knowledge of gift planning. They are more comfortable with accounting than counting. How are you going to break through with them?

2. Board members and donors who provide the most support have limited tolerance for numbers; yet do have a strong desire to understand the big picture. They don't understand why they shouldn't be able to see their own executed gift in the organization's campaign report unless it was made in cash.

They are asking for more than you can tell them about how your campaign works and what drives success.

3.  No one knows how to report total dollars raised for different types of gifts. There is no standard approach. The concept of Total Financial Resource Development (explained more fully in **Chapter Five**) has not gained broad acceptance or is still in its introduction phase.

4.  You are asked, "What is your planned giving program worth?" and, "What will it achieve?" but you don't have a good answer.

5.  Since the fundraising scandals of 9/11 (ever-close in the rear view mirror), donors have been demanding increasing levels of accountability from charitable organizations. IRS Form 990 reports were not as widely available in those days. You feel a need for more granularity in your fundraising reports to show fundraising up in some areas and down in others.

6.  You encounter a problem that is vexing for both fundraisers and donors: lack of incentive or even a disincentive for acquiring gifts that don't count in the short-term, but that will be very significant later. Conventional contribution reports categorically do not recognize the fundraising achievements that often lead to the largest gifts, i.e., irrevocable and revocable commitments.

7.  You sense a "quarterly report mentality" with little investment in the future. How can you rally your true stakeholders to a long-term vision when the priority seems always on the immediate result?

8.  Fundraising software in use today still does not enable CEOs or boards to see how planned gifts are actually a part of their current fundraising results. When will there be a panel on the home page where gift officers can see at a glance, for example, the achievements from revocable gifts or the full transfers for gift annuities that are often ignored because they are invisible and lumped together with other gifts? Pipeline reports do not include important sources of future gifts or identify a ready market of likely donors.

9. You have no way to image or visualize results or trends because they are obscured by the One Number. No alternative views are available to see year-to-year campaign dynamics. No qualitative analysis seems possible.

10. Fundraising professionals who are particularly adept in gift planning go unrecognized because their signal achievements are treated as "money over the transom" and not included in annual reporting. The most successful fundraisers leave for greener pastures.

My efforts to provide multidimensional counting and reporting for my own organizational managers eventually led me to be involved in the Partnership for Philanthropic Planning's ("PPP") national task force that issued the best practice for counting all charitable gifts—the PPP Guidelines for Reporting and Counting Charitable Gifts. In my own work, following that practice has enabled us to profile our campaign initially just for a single year, and then over time. It guided our gift-marketing strategy through the turbulent years of the 2008-2011 recession. And eventually, our multidimensional counting practices led us to design new gifts across the traditional silos of annual/major/planned giving, opening up the world of personalized philanthropy discussed in earlier chapters.

As simple as this concept sounds, I never realized it might be possible to proactively design a gift this way (umbrella agreements in multiple dimensions—sometimes called blended gifts) before getting engaged in the questions about counting and reporting gifts in the big picture. So, I believe this approach must have grown organically out of that experience, at least for me. I can imagine the whole process being reversed for fundraisers reading this book. One or two great "origin stories" with donors who seek impact through personalized philanthropy will be the catalyst for a revision of counting practices, gift acceptance policies, and other organizational pronouncements that can stand in the way of transformative gifts.

In addition to management reporting and gift structuring, multidimensional counting also helps us as individual fundraisers to give a good answer to that vexing question I mentioned earlier—how much did you raise? Fear of evaluation has to be tops on the list for most planned gift officers, for the exact reason that much of what they do, or feel they should do as planned gift officers (i.e., securing the future), has not been countable in their organizations. The default financial measures actually create disincentives for fundraisers to pursue the kinds of gifts that build the pipeline, because they are invisible in our evaluations and measures of achievement.

The cumulative impact of reporting solely on One Number is a primary reason that all philanthropy is not personalized philanthropy: One Number just can't capture the breadth and depth of what the most ardent donors are trying to do with their gifts. Excluding irrevocable and revocable commitments from reportable fundraising achievement, and relying solely on One Number, marginalizes an entire universe of gifts—including planned gifts—and in so doing promotes the fragmented approach to fundraising that we call silos.

## Define Yourself

Without *us* defining what is important to be measured, there are plenty of other people who will do it for us. If you want to define yourself rather than be defined by others, you need to have another way— preferably a multidimensional approach—that reflects what you are actually trying to achieve. There are three structural supports to a fully donor-focused, personalized development effort: gift acceptance policies, policies for setting fundraising goals and counting gifts toward those goals, and policies for crediting gifts for the purpose of evaluating fundraiser achievement. When these policies focus on bookable gifts, they form the backbone of a siloed development department, where annual gifts, major current gifts, and planned gifts (and the fundraisers responsible for them) are never encouraged—or allowed—to work together.

**observation**

Besides the CPAs, CFOs, and CEOs, there were, and are, other *people who count*, as well: our donors and our fundraisers. So how do we talk about our numbers to them? And what measures do we want to use to gauge our own effectiveness? Is there a possibility for a common shared language that conveys the weight and breadth of what we really do? Yes: The PPP guidelines provide that shared approach for understanding the impact of gifts and the effectiveness of fundraisers.

Rather than thinking about the PPP guidelines as if they were issued in a monolithic way and set in stone tablets many years ago, I think it more productive to look at them as if they were just released today. Maybe it's a bit of a stretch, but they really are a kind of manifesto: the very first platform or mission statement specifically intended to advance the art and practice of donor-focused fundraising and philanthropy, at least with regard to counting and reporting.

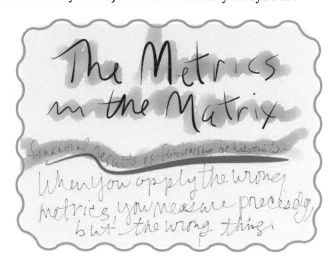

The prime directive—the boldest and best assertion of the PPP guidelines—is still its simplest: It is never appropriate to report only One Number when announcing campaign results. Be very clear about this: You are *not* trying to replace the financials your CFO uses with your accountant, your board, or your bank. There is no substitute for FASB or audited financial statements. They are authoritative. Whatever system you develop has to reconcile with that and be built upon the same basic truths if it is to have any credibility or validity with your stakeholders, your "people who count." However, they are *financial* reports. You are developing a report about *fundraising achievements*. Your measures of effectiveness are different and describe the truth from different perspectives and for different purposes. *Counting and not accounting*, it's sometimes said. Your CFO should be your best friend when it comes to understanding results, or you will be nowhere.

If your organization were to adopt the PPP guidelines, what would change and what would your reporting then look like?

## Three Dimensions of Charitable Giving

The PPP guidelines' essential core principle is that the best way to count and report gifts is by using a system that reflects the same classifications as people use when they actually make their own gifts. Using this approach, what can we observe that we would not have been able to see before? We see that just three categories fit the bill and are easily represented: cash/outright gifts; irrevocable gifts; and revocable commitments.

Category 1. Cash or equivalent contributions, counted in full on financial reports:

- ◆ outright gifts, appreciated securities

- ◆ funds from bequests received

- ◆ pledges, with reference to short-term payable e.g., three to five years

- ◆ testamentary pledges, with reference to payable on death or long-term foundation pledges

Category 2. Irrevocable gifts, counted in part on financial reports:

- ◆ Charitable trusts

- ◆ Charitable gift annuities

- ◆ Other irrevocable gifts

Category 3. Revocable commitments, counted not at all on financial reports:

- ◆ Bequests with specified amounts

- ◆ Bequests without specified amounts

- ◆ Other revocable gifts

| | Three Categories of Gifts | Fiscal Year 20__ |
|---|---|---|
| 1 | **Cash or Equivalent Contributions** | |
| | ◆ Outright gifts of cash (does not include income received from CRTs and CGAs reported in category 2 or payments on pledges) | 20,624 |
| | ◆ Legacies and bequests (cash received from planned gifts | 16,791 |
| | ◆ Pledges (except testamentary) | 26,065 |
| | ◆ Testamentary pledges (planned estate gifts) | 24,800 |
| | Total cash and pledges | 88,280 |
| 2 | **Irrevocable (Life Income) Gifts** | |
| | ◆ Charitable remainder trusts (CRTs) | 2,263 |
| | ◆ Charitable gift annuities (CGAs) | 1,278 |
| | ◆ Other irrevocable gifts | 0 |
| | Total irrevocable gifts | 3,541 |
| 3 | **Document Commitments** | |
| | ◆ Gifts with specified amounts | 625 |
| | ◆ Gifts with amounts not specified (e.g., percentage) | 4,632 |
| | Total commitments estimated | 5,257 |
| | **Total Financial Resource Development** | 97,078 |

The simple categorization made possible by the PPP guidelines—representing gifts in the three dimensions corresponding to the ways donors think about and actually create their gifts—opens up enormous possibilities for understanding your fundraising in depth and detail that you might not have thought of.

The Guidelines are good. You've got data. It depicts the unfiltered results at face value showing what gift planners actually achieve. A great deal of transparency and clarity is gained by having a system that allows a donor who had contributed $25,000 for a gift annuity to see that actual number represented in our "score card." That was certainly better than explaining that only the charitable deduction for the gift would count and be a part of the One Number.

But why were gift annuities good that particular year, or especially bad? Or, for that matter, how many new known expectancies (revocable gifts) might you need to add to your pipeline in order to maintain a certain level of revenues from bequests actually received? Are there trends we should be watching and doing something about? Would we be able to effect change by strategically using our marketing effort, and would we be able to detect that in our results? Now we are asking a different question, beyond "what's the count?"

## Organizational MRIs—The Inner Life of Your Campaign

How can you be an activist in your own shop and *use* the data, instead of just passively counting and reporting the numbers? I like to think of the reports you can generate as organizational MRIs or CT scans, because they can reveal the inner workings of your campaign in a way that was not possible before. You can get an in-depth understanding—see the dynamics of your campaign.

Over time, you can see the impact of economic highs and lows on your campaign. What's most important is that you can manage more strategically because you can see the impact of major marketing initiatives and business decisions that have an effect on the type of gifts donors choose to make. You can make understanding the results part of your fundraising conversation.

These simple charts are just to illustrate the point. Your campaign will likely look much different.

### *Total Financial Resource Development (TFRD)*

This following chart shows graphically the entire campaign in a given year. It's perfect for the numerically challenged or for those who have a more visual learning style. You don't need to know the numbers to see the trends and impacts. On your own charts, you can see the impact of the gifts made by individuals, and we even list some of their names to remind us as we look back over time.

Please note that for the charts in this book, I'll be removing some of the details you might wish to include in your own. This is not to make them

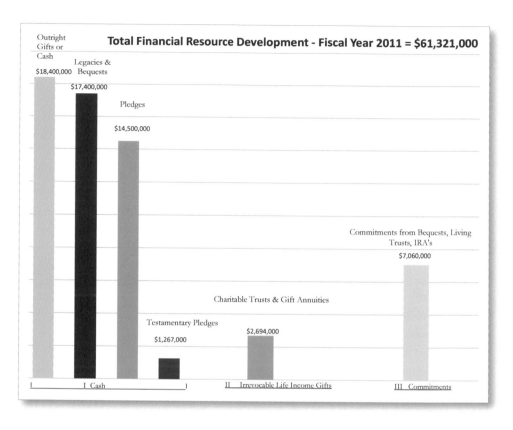

appear more anonymous, but because you don't really need to see the numbers to get the trends being discussed.

In the above chart, you can clearly see the three categories of gifts—outright/irrevocable/revocable—each reported at face value, along with the subcategories. Of special interest, of course, is Category 1, since all of these gifts are going to be reportable and visible on most financial reports. The difference is that in the conventional reports, you will only see One Number.

In these reports, especially in Category 1, you can see contributions from different types of gifts in granular detail as subcategories. For instance, you can see reportable gifts of cash (including appreciated securities), revenues that have been received from bequests and short-term pledges, and pledges that are payable on death. You can use this data in a lot of interesting ways.

For example, most donors think of the campaign as we have taught them: One Number. But you can easily see how cash and pledges differ, and you can see the impact of bequests received in any given year. When we answer the question, "how much did you raise," with One Number, many donors believe that all of those funds are expendable for the purpose of the mission in that same year. Clearly, with pledges being a significant source, that is not the case. It is also true that many, if not most, of the bequests reported here in Category 1 were executed and signed off on in prior years. Seeing the connection between the documented commitments in Category 3 and the bequests received in Category 1 is the beginning of understanding what this important part of the major gift pipeline is all about.

During this particular down economic year, donors seemed to have been more shy about both testamentary pledges and gifts of cash from securities. In succeeding years, these numbers both rose as donors began to have more confidence and the stock market nearly doubled to new highs, surpassing the previous years' lows.

### *Development Activity by Region*

On the next page is another view of the same year, but showing a number of different fundraisers and regions.

You can see how each fundraiser or region tends to have a different strength or its own portfolio of gifts. In any given year, one fundraiser may do very well with one type of gift, ranging from a long-term pledge to a new known expectancy.

You can see how some gift officers seem to do better with older donors, raising bequest expectancies or pledges payable upon death. Others seem to specialize in pledges. There is a texture to a campaign that would be completely lost or invisible without the ability to see results in multiple dimensions.

Expectancies did very well in 2011 in our national region, where we made a big push for this type of gift during the down economic years. During those years, we believed that donors would still be open to including us in their estate plans, perhaps as an alternative to an outright gift that year; or perhaps their professional advisors cautioned them about making long-term commitments till the economy righted itself again.

Following the PPP guidelines allows you to track your fundraising in a novel, granular way. You can see the story of the shifting economy or your

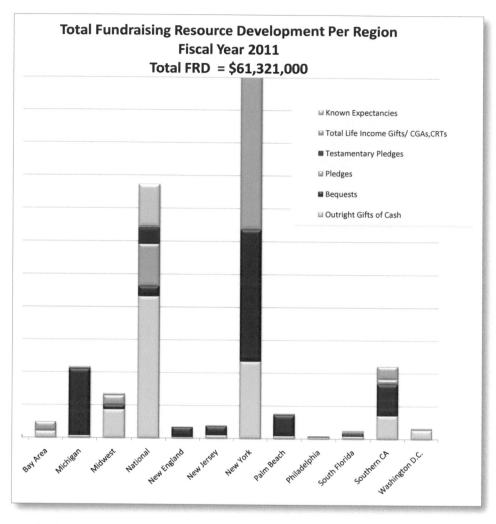

marketing program, even your strengths and weaknesses, playing out over time in whatever charts you happen to look at.

You can't tell much about your campaign from just one year, and these charts give you the ability to envision your program over an extended frame of reference. The more years of experience you can look at and correlate with happenings in the economy and in your own organization's history, the better you will be able to tell a meaningful story about your big picture.

### Revocable Commitments

The story of known expectancies (see chart on facing page) is always an interesting one, especially because this level of detail is completely

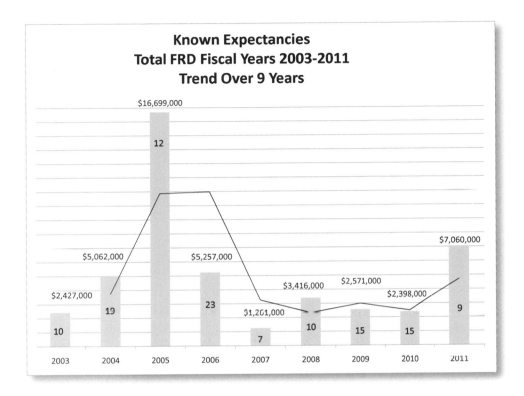

Known Expectancies
Total FRD Fiscal Years 2003-2011
Trend Over 9 Years

invisible in most financial reports, where known expectancies are typically not counted. Here you can see years in which we had great gains from gifts that had to be structured as revocable. During the early years of the down economy revocable gifts took a hit, but then actually increased.

This was not an accident. While we knew we would have trouble with cash and appreciated asset gifts in those down years, we paid special attention to this area. We believed we had a shot to increase gifts during a time when we would begin focusing more intentionally on building relationships with our most ardent donors. More than just riding out the down economy, we could actively try to prepare the ground for a stronger recovery.

### Bequests Actually Received

There is, or ought to be, no more interesting story to tell than comparing your pipeline of known expectancies (revocable gifts) with your experience of bequests actually received. (See chart on next page.)

While this might be pure speculation, the number of bequests actually received is consistently about a third of the new known expectancies.

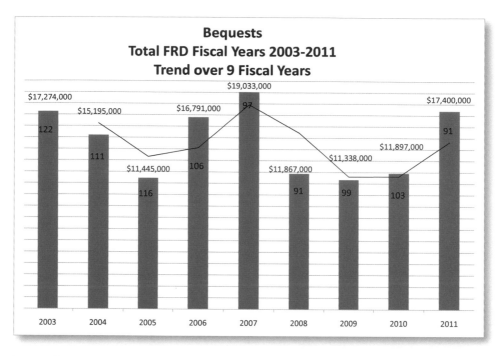

**Bequests**
**Total FRD Fiscal Years 2003-2011**
**Trend over 9 Fiscal Years**

Does that suggest a minimum level of known expectancies to strive for? Who knows? But you do know for certain that you will need to market and acquire new bequest expectancies in order to achieve them. Of greater importance is that during the years of the down economy, bequests received did *not* track the economy, and actually rose. As with many other institutions, during those years we found ourselves afloat on a cushion of bequests.

### Long-term and Testamentary Pledges

Another key element of Category 1 (the category that shows fully bookable gifts) is long-term and testamentary pledges. The PPP guidelines recommend that there should be a distinction between pledges that would normally be payable in just a few years, and those made typically by older donors that would not be payable until the death of the donor. That has proven to be a very valuable distinction because it allowed us to promote and design gifts for a small but very significant part of our constituency— older donors engaged in estate planning. It has also been very persuasive in illustrating the value of the PPP guidelines and charts such as these.

Irrevocable pledges (both long and short-term) are so important because, in conventional campaign counting, they are generally reported the same as cash. (See the chart below.) It is essentially a way to count irrevocable gift commitments that were legally binding pledges, with the longer-term schedules done as part of a donor's estate planning.

There was some controversy about this, because not every charitable organization accepts or promotes such gifts. However, for many organizations these commitments come from the most ardent supporters who have already included the charity in their estate plans. Since they have been engaged for many years already and have often made many gifts, they feel comfortable about pledging a portion of the gift they have already included as part of their estates. Such gifts are often vital to the success of a campaign. These gifts come from those who lead.

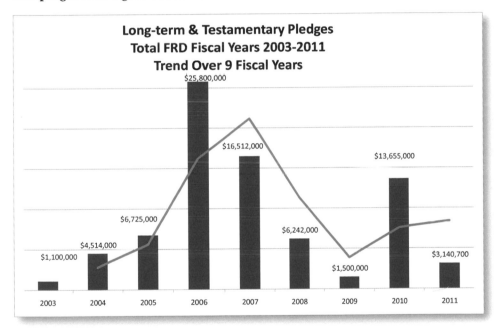

There is an interesting story that could be told about this chart. It shows the beginning of the timeline when such testamentary gifts were first being promoted to major gift donors by the American Committee for the Weizmann Institute of Science. It took several years for this kind of gift to catch on. But then these gifts became the major source of growth for us. When the down economy happened, there was a falling off of such gifts, which I think reflected donors' lack of confidence during those years. But, as the economy began to pick up, several major donors stepped up with leadership gifts that were testamentary pledges, and the category has begun to recover.

You could tell a different story, but our organizational "MRI" supports this version. It is a great way to have a conversation with donors, to let them see how their leadership in giving truly makes a difference and shapes the entire campaign. We often say that it is only a few gifts that make a difference in a campaign. Now we can show it: Sometimes it will be outright gifts, sometimes a bequest, and sometimes even testamentary pledges. Tracking your campaign in this way, you will know precisely what made the difference.

### *Life Income Gifts*

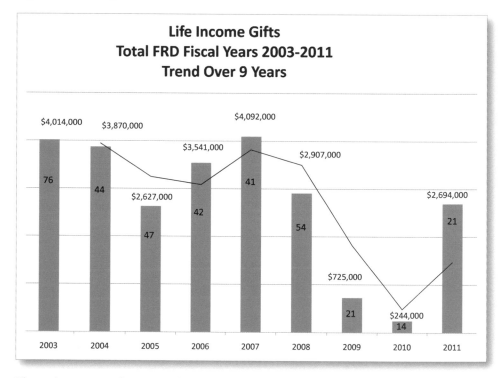

There is not much to say about charitable gift annuities ("CGAs"). (See the chart above.) Most organizations see them as a critical part of their traditional planned giving program. In this chart of several years' activity, you can see them rise and fall. They rise when the rates change and our marketing hints that this is the last chance to lock in at a high rate, or the last chance to lock in before the rates fall.

CGAs take a big tumble during an economic downturn because they seem very sensitive to economic changes, at least initially. But then they come back, as donors seem to seek a return to "quality," which might mean they choose gifts that offer some security through providing a fixed income that will not change over their lifetime.

### *Legacies as a Part of Contribution Income*

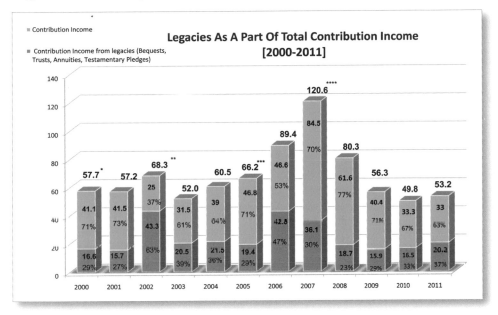

People "count" in more than one way. Some people are counting and evaluating our work, such as the CFO. Other people "count" because they matter to the organization and us. There are many different kinds of stakeholders and they all count something, or for something.

So, what matters most to your CFO and CEO? When you are trying to interest them in an alternative donor-focused way to count and report, as an adjunct to FASB, what do you want them to consider? What would matter most to them? I would propose a chart (see chart above) that combines the two ways of reporting: the One Number and the Total FRD method suggested by the PPP guidelines. I would show them what matters most to them: contribution income. If you can show your people who count that planned gifts consistently make up, say, 30 percent of your total revenues, you've begun to make a pretty convincing case for paying attention to them, and to you.

Here are all the gifts that *do* count in the One Number, broken out by type.

If you want to show the impact of planned gifts on your current numbers, it looks a lot like this.

What we're singling out here are all the Category 1 gifts. Those are the bookable planned gifts in Blue, and the others that are not planned gifts. If you were just looking at One Number, you wouldn't know any of this. Note: Revocable gifts and portions of gift annuities not included here.

### *Planned Giving Inventory*

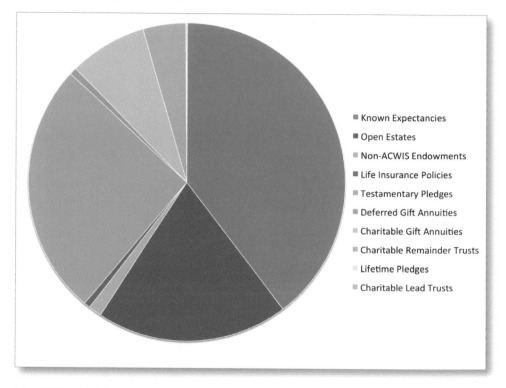

- Known Expectancies
- Open Estates
- Non-ACWIS Endowments
- Life Insurance Policies
- Testamentary Pledges
- Deferred Gift Annuities
- Charitable Gift Annuities
- Charitable Remainder Trusts
- Lifetime Pledges
- Charitable Lead Trusts

The PPP guidelines can provide you with a technology to understand the impacts on campaign in greater detail. But they can only begin to convey a sense how planned giving matters to the organization's future. When a board member asks, "What is your program really worth?" this is an opportunity to prepare a planned giving inventory. (See chart above.)

A planned giving inventory provokes a conversation about what happens after a donor makes a planned gift commitment.

Two possibilities:

1. The gift was irrevocable, so the contribution has already been recorded in the campaign, though the money has not yet been received.

2. The gift was revocable, so it has not yet been recorded as a contribution, and will only be booked upon its receipt, usually maturing upon the death of the donor.

How do you keep track of these revocable gifts? From talking to many people about this, it seems the answer is, usually, *you don't*—until they mature. A planned giving inventory is probably the best approach to convey to your stakeholders a sense of what is to come in the future. Many gift officers are very surprised on first taking inventory, because they had no idea of the magnitude of what had come before them. All those precomputer 3 x 5 cards about gift expectancies that were never recorded can be brought into your view.

The term "inventory" here serves more a fundraising purpose than a financial purpose, but it can be useful in tracking the funds, as well as in providing a market for major gifts to come. It is essential to validate each of the entries and keep the inventory up to date, as gifts mature and are removed, and new gifts are added. It is the sensible thing to do to keep a list of donors who have you in their plans, and to keep in touch on a regular basis. But it doesn't always happen. A planned giving inventory is a straightforward list of all such completed planned gifts from which revenues have not yet been received. It can also be constructed so that it records only those gifts that have not yet been booked in previous years. When validated and the donors are engaged, it becomes a true pipeline of future major gifts.

The results can seem dramatic because, as one fundraising executive commented, as impressive as this inventory of future gifts may be, it only represents a small percentage of the gifts that we are likely to receive.

### What Came Out of the PPP Guidelines? An Idea that Won't Go Away

Adoption of the PPP guidelines was a challenge to the status quo. You might say it was one of the first battles waged and won on behalf of donor-focused giving. So what, if anything, has come out of the PPP guidelines? Have they really changed our world?

I think the answer is both yes, and no.

*Yes*, in the sense that calling attention to the concept of donor-focused *anything* helped bring more light on the synthetic and artificial quality of our conventional financial effectiveness measures. It helped draw a distinction between the multidimensional approach and everything else that was *not* donor-focused. Perhaps much more importantly for me personally, it helped set the stage in my own gift practice for another development later on: *the potential not just for counting gifts in multidimensions, but for shaping and designing gifts in an entirely new, full-spectrum, and donor-focused way.* The previous chapters of this book are devoted to this transformational aspect of personalized philanthropy.

*No*, in that while a donor-focused approach made an appearance and emerged as a wave of new culture, most organizations still focus solely on counting and reporting the One Number. The institution-focused culture still defines the balance and overshadows donor-focused fundraising in most respects.

Why Yes and No? Fundamentally, the matter is still unsettled between institutional and donor-focused cultures. As younger donors approach the age where they are considered to be prospects for planned giving, each organization will have to make its own shift in its own way to a more personalized philanthropy. While it may be a quiet revolution, it is important. It's a wave, if not a tidal force, running through the history of philanthropy.

To have these two cultures going at it is really not all that bad. In fact, it's actually an improvement, compared to having the donor-focused culture completely submerged so as to stay under the radar. The PPP guidelines for Counting and Reporting Charitable Gifts were probably the first fully realized wave of donor-focused personalized philanthropy. These guidelines continue to grow and evolve. They carry some essence of an idea that just won't go away.

In addition to the One Number that FASB or financial statements provide, we now have other numbers that are more accurate leading indicators of our success. For example, the number of testamentary pledges acquired, or the number or dollars actually received from bequests, compared to dollars from cash/outright gifts. Perhaps the One Number with the greatest potential impact we should have been looking at all along was known expectancies. One Number might not be so bad, IF you can choose which number you want to look at! It is just the tyranny of *the* One Number that is the problem.

Now there are new profiling and screening techniques that can give us not only masses of data to help us understand our campaigns in their entirety, but to enlighten us about individual donors, one at a time. We should be able to see "at a glance" any individual donor's giving history along with

## Why Do We Count All Gifts, Not Just Planned Ones?

Members of the PPP Task Force that developed the PPP guidelines were more prescient than they could have known. Most will not even recall that they overran their original charter! They were charged solely with examining counting guidelines for planned gifts. But, very quickly and with hardly anyone taking notice, the task force drew up an entirely new agenda. It was, "Where do planned gifts fit in the big picture?"

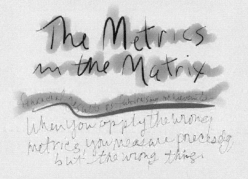

Their final recommendations on how all types of charitable gifts should be counted and reported went head-to-head *against* the Council on Advancement and Support of Education's ("CASE") Management Reporting Standards, which were generally accepted by educational institutions and widely used outside the education sector as well. In 2005, when the first edition of the PPP guidelines were issued, the CASE standard counted irrevocable gifts at discounted present value and did not count revocable gifts at all. CASE was solidly behind the reporting of One Number, and worked hard to calculate all kinds of gifts into a roughly equivalent "current dollars" form for that purpose. In the current (2009) edition of the Management Reporting Standards, CASE recommends including revocable gifts in campaign totals at face value if they are pledged during the campaign, documented, and reported separately from outright gifts and irrevocable deferred gifts.

Irrevocable deferred gifts may be included in campaign totals at face value, but both face and discounted present values should be reported. The Association of Fundraising Professionals has endorsed the PPP guidelines as well.

**food for thought**

## A Challenge to the Powers that Be in Fundraising Software Design

*As I close this chapter on counting and reporting, together with the publisher of this "In the Trenches" series, I want to offer a serious challenge to fundraising software companies.*

I recently learned that for more than ten years, as part of product marketing, some fundraising software companies have been referencing source material on reporting and counting charitable gifts in their marketing materials, including an article I wrote with Bill Samers for *The Journal of Gift Planning*, "Planned Giving in the Big Picture: Talking about your numbers to people who count." (See the **Appendix** for a resource list that includes this article.)

Being cited by big donor services companies was extremely flattering, at first. Things I'd written were being introduced to many new readers who might be having their first exposure to more holistic counting concepts. It was great news that software companies seemed to understand what this is all about, but at the same time, it was a disappointment.

When you understand and also have the capability, don't you also have a responsibility to act? In one step, unilaterally, a single software company taking the lead could change the face of fundraising forever, simply by institutionalizing the donor-focused vision, right alongside the institution-focused vision.

If it is worth marketing, then isn't it worth doing? Why, then, are you lagging behind in bringing these tools to the marketplace?

So the challenge is to implement for all your customers a set of individualized profiles that includes for each donor the essential Total FRD donor profile, showing lifetime gifts in all three categories from the PPP guidelines— outright gifts, irrevocable gifts and revocable gifts. Only in this way will fundraisers be able to recognize at a glance each donor's giving history and future intentions in a holistic, full-spectrum, and personalized way.

More than ten years have passed since the concepts were developed and national fundraising guidelines adopted and approved. The technology is mature. The time is now. Without this infrastructure built in to fundraising software, it will be impossible to institutionalize this multidimensional and holistic understanding of donors and how they give. With it, you could change the giving world.

**A Challenge**

> ## On Your Way to a Donor Today? Run a Total FRD Profile First!
>
> It's a great idea to know your donor's giving history before you get there, but your software might show just "cash." You could be missing all the good stuff. If you can't run a profile like this with your software, it is worth it to do it yourself. But please call them for me and say, "Shame on you."
>
> | Total FRD Profile | $305,000 |
> |---|---|
> | Contribution Income | 30,000 |
> | 1. Cash/pledges/outright | 5,000 |
> | 2. Life income gifts (irrevocable) | 50,000 |
> | 3. Bequest (revocable) | 250,000 |

any of their known future giving intentions. An enterprising gift officer may choose to pursue this information, but it is often available deep in a file or database. Clearly this approach has not been institutionalized. As a matter of best practices, why are we not using it?

## To Recap

◆ There is a strong connection between an organization's counting policies and the gifts that fundraisers pursue. Personalized philanthropy flourishes in an organization that sets goals, counts gifts, and credits fundraisers in a multidimensional way. It can be smothered under metrics that may be precise but measure less than what's wanted. Beware the metrics of the Matrix.

◆ Planned gifts are one part of the big picture for your donors and for your overall fundraising results. The *full* picture involves all of an individual's giving over time.

◆ Counting can and should be reconciled with accounting, but they are distinct processes with different purposes. Personalized philanthropy provides an opportunity to improve communication with the CFO who is just as much a stakeholder in success as you are.

# Chapter Six

## Being the Change:
## Using This Book to Make Your Own Shift

### IN THIS CHAPTER

···→ Where were you when the last silo died?

···→ How do you institutionalize donor-focused fundraising?

···→ Where is the *next* generation of gift planners coming from, and would you hire one?

At the beginning, I said that this book would likely turn out to be more bio than info. I wanted to write about the journey gift officers make when going through the shift from institution-focused fundraising to donor-focused philanthropy.

The original working title of the book referred to making the shift to donor-focused giving as a "quiet revolution." While it's not as quiet as it once was, it has been much more of a person-centered journey than an institutional one. Institutions haven't changed all that much, but I think individuals can and have.

These Matrix-crashing concepts have tested patience, persistence and passion. Will these ideas strike a chord with you and your fellow gift officers and donors and continue to evolve in the wild? I suppose we'll just have to wait and see.

I used the analogy of the movie, The Matrix, as an experiment in writing this book. At first, it struck me as the best way to try to explain and highlight the stark differences between the two cultures of fundraising. I wondered how far I could push the Matrix analogy before it might break down. As it turns out, the analogy goes much farther than I thought it would, but it doesn't go all the way.

In the end, the dominant culture is still the one most familiar to us— institution-focused and often bureaucracy-bound. More typically than we would like, it is a system with many channels that separate fundraisers—and donors, too— artificially into divisions by the type of gift they should ask for, usually an annual, major, or planned gift. What defines the identity of staff in such organizations more often than not is their programmatic quest for that one type of gift, even to the exclusion of others.

The donor-focused culture is the one I'm attempting to convey as an alternative. It is more organic and connected with the donor. It keeps reminding you of the "donor's compelling interest." The culture and the process of gift design is based on exploring the possibilities for creating gifts in the particular space where the compelling interests of donors meet the equally compelling institutional needs and priorities. It is a discovery culture, driven as much by curiosity as fundraising.

I also think the donor-focused culture is somewhat disorderly and improvisational, because the full spectrum of philanthropic building blocks is always on the table and, after all, that's where the donors are!

The primary shift taking place from one culture to the other is in the transition from the 'selling' of a gift vehicle, to engaging and meeting donors "where they are." Ultimately, this is an art, which means that the enterprising gift officer has to be a risk-taker, an explorer working in unknown territory, often without a map. You can't always know where you will go, but you can know where to begin.

Pushing the Matrix analogy a little further, the possibilities for working in one culture differ markedly from the other. The institution-focused culture is largely blind to the donor-focused culture. In the movie, the occupants are enslaved, without realizing it. Where staff in the institution-focused development office are often bound and programmed, gift officers who escape the Matrix and operate under principles of personalized philanthropy are free and more improvisational in their practice. They have the full spectrum of gifts to work with and the entire lifetimes of the donors to consider. Instead of deferring planned gifts, they start working today. Their idea of fun is to accelerate both mission impact and donor satisfaction. In the typical development office, where annual, major, and planned gifts are in competition, this would be impossible.

In the movie *The Matrix,* certain "organic" characters (they are people, as opposed to programs) famously gain a kind of special access and insight into their world and themselves when they begin to understand the true nature of their artificial Matrix environment. So it is in the alternative fundraising culture, that *personalized philanthropy gift officers can use old tools in new ways.* Able to be resourceful in their own right or to call upon powerful guiding teams, they can also *design entirely new ways of navigating throughout the system,* crossing (and crashing) boundaries between annual/major/planned gift disciplines, and beyond, to get things done. Under personalized philanthropy, the building blocks of philanthropy really have not changed, but how we can use them certainly has.

## Preparing Your Own Shift

The subtitle of the book suggests "Making the Real Shift to Donor-Focused Giving." So I've asked myself, and I'm asking you now: what are the key things that need to shift?

Here is what I think we must shift in order to move closer to a personalized philanthropy model:

1. Let's finally shift the way we count gifts, to include all three dimensions of giving (outright, irrevocable, and revocable), and let's place higher expectations on our software companies to help us be smarter about how we portray our donors.

Let's count it all and let's see it all: what counts in fundraising, as well as what counts in the financials. If you and your organization are really donor-focused, why not show the whole donor, from both the institution's perspective and the donor's perspective? Is it simply because we don't want to see what we can't count? That's not a good enough reason anymore. Software companies can help us rise to the challenge and advance philanthropy for all.

2. Let's shift how the development office thinks about development and the development office.

   Did you know that there are medical development offices that have separated fundraising divisions according to the parts of the body? While the development office is becoming more fragmented, the new field of personalized medicine has turned a corner and is treating the whole person, rather than just the part of the body where problem symptoms appear. Can fundraising learn anything from science? If you were starting over, would you aim to create a fundraising system that would fragment and demean its supporters in a completely impersonal and diabolical way? Let's rethink this.

3. Let's prepare the next generation of gift officers as enlightened generalists.

   Instead of preparing a generation trained as highly disciplined order-takers for annual, major, and planned gifts, let's cultivate a more creative if somewhat disorderly group that is better prepared for a broader challenge. Let's break the mold and teach a generation how to relish and create smart gifts that balance both the compelling needs of donors and the compelling needs of our institutions.

In *The Matrix* movie series, the good guys finally win. The people defeat the machines. Human culture is restored and once again flourishes. However, in our real fundraising world, the Matrix analogy finally does break. The good guys from personalized philanthropy will never quite defeat institution-focused fundraising. The reason is that they were never enemies in the first place.

In truth, we need to care about *both* donor-focused philanthropy and institution-focused fundraising. Most especially, we need to care that they are in balance. We need to be able to first recognize and then be able to move between the two worlds, to help both our donors and our institutions. *If there is any real chance for the success of donor-focused philanthropy, it is that the people who read this book will become more aware and more adept—not only in working with their donors but in working with their institutions and becoming leaders.*

After you read this book, I hope your belief will grow in a wave of strong new gift officers—a next generation practicing personalized philanthropy who will in fact become the future leaders of major institutions. That way, if we don't have an outright victory, we can hope for something even better: a take-over from inside.

### Three Pillars of Personalized Philanthropy: A Message in a Bottle for Donors

What are the lessons donors can teach us about personalized philanthropy? What questions can we consider when approaching our own gifts? How do these donor parables relate to your own philanthropy?

Hopefully this book has raised as many questions as it has answered, and then some. To provide some insight into my own thinking and the questions I've asked, here are three lessons that I have learned from the donors referenced throughout the book. I think you will find that these lessons permeate all of the examples and help inform the shaping and design of each of the gift plans, matched to the interests of the individual donors and to the compelling needs of the organizations they care about. To me, these questions and insights point to better ways to do effective philanthropy, powered by personalized gift design.

I like to think of the three pillars as a forgotten fragment—a message in a bottle—written by a philanthropist long ago. It was floated in the hope it would be found by people who want to make a plan but too often have come up against the crush of reality: "Life is what happens when you're busy making other plans" (John Lennon). "Everybody has a plan until they get punched in the face" (Mike Tyson). Whether you are a philanthropist or a fundraiser, this message resonates for people seeking to understand and act on their charitable impulse. This message in a bottle seems relevant all year long, at any soulful season of giving.

Imagine that you found the bottle and read this message:

1. *Give with a warm hand.* My friend said it was better to give with a warm hand than a cold one. She meant it, and did it. Maybe you've heard the phrase from Warren Buffett, "Giving While Living." Giving with a warm hand is the big idea behind that. It also shapes The Giving Pledge, which has encouraged so many philanthropists to designate at least half of their estates for helping others. So, if you feel charitable, it's up to you to decide what you want to happen with your gift. Go ahead and make your statement. You do not have to defer or leave this important life-defining decision to someone else.

2. *Give with a warm heart.* Besides giving while living, you can give as you live, with passion and a warm heart. Share that. Do something meaningful to you. Start now. Aim high. Scale up and go long. Make a habit of giving. You can achieve much more by combining current gifts with future gifts for something important to you. Most charities will allow you to target or restrict your gift. The really enlightened ones encourage it. You can start with something doable now and yet grow the impact of your support with each additional gift.

3. *Give with a cool head.* Give smart. Not just from your heart. Employ the powerful tools of *personalized philanthropy* and smart advisors who can show you how. It's possible and even okay to benefit your loved ones and yourself from your giving: bequests, charitable trusts, gift annuities, charitable insurance, and retirement plans—especially bequests. Find out about virtual endowments and how to build equity in your endowment. This way, you can create a lasting legacy, and it can begin now.

## When You Have Made that Shift to Personalized Philanthropy

Once you grasp the basic concepts of personalized gift design and especially the three killer apps, you will have both the tools and the facility to develop your own gift designs—plans that work both for the institutions and the donors you care about.

*These are the gifts that will be uniquely identified with your own practice. They are your legacy.*

At that time, when you are well along your way to making the shift, the fundraising Matrix will fall away. You will see the synthetic structures, silos, and boundaries of your fundraising development office for what they are. Maybe you won't be able to see through walls or fly through space, but you *will* be able to operate as an effective agent, trusted by both donor and institution. You will conduct your gift practice in an entirely new way with new forms that you yourself will have had a part in shaping, traversing the boundaries of annual, major and planned gifts. Your practice will recenter itself. Instead of focusing on gift vehicles, you will be helping both your donors and your organization to achieve something of great moment.

The right gifts, for the right donors, for the right times. With the greatest possible impact and recognition. Starting right now.

# Afterword

I n my professional role as the dean of The Wallace Chair in Philanthropy at The American College, I teach advisors and fundraisers how to collaborate better to serve high capacity donors and clients. In escaping from the "Matrix" silos of annual, major, and planned gifts and by concentrating on how to achieve the high-capacity donor's compelling interests aligned with your organization's compelling needs, you are thinking as would the best client advisors. And you bring to the planning table a realm of expertise that very few advisors understand or appreciate.

To see the opportunity, let me outline how the best advisors today see a legacy plan. You will see in this account what may be missing in your process, but you will also see what is missing in the advisor's process that you can complete.

A good legacy advisor working with a married donor, say, age fifty-five who has, say, $15 million in net worth, has grown children, and who has significant noncash assets, will begin with questions to elicit client goals, dreams, and aspirations. Among the questions might be these:

◆ How much is enough for you and your spouse? Now? At retirement?

◆ At your death there are only three places wealth can go, to taxes, heirs, or charity.

◆ How much is enough for the children? How much might be too much?

◆ Having taken care of the heirs, would you like to reduce taxes in favor of charity?

The advisor then organizes the plan so that the client's financial needs are met throughout the client's lifetime, come what may, taking into account investment returns, and the possible contingencies of disability, sickness, or premature death. In a well-made plan, "enough," as the client defines that, goes to heirs, whether during the parent's life, or at their death, and the taxable estate may go to, say, a private foundation. Perhaps in this case $10 million might go to heirs, and $5 million might go at death to a private foundation, and zero would be due in estate taxes. Seeing such a testamentary plan a client may ask, "Could I start sooner? If I am going to leave $5 million to charity anyway, why not start sooner? I would enjoy it more and could see the good it does. I could involve my children. I could make a difference while alive."

Advisors sometimes speak of "social capital" as the money that wealthy clients are devoting to social good, whether involuntarily (taxes) or voluntarily. The goal of planning, then, is to shift social capital from involuntary philanthropy to voluntary. In such a tax-centric legacy plan, social capital is just the money planners rescue from taxes and generally store up in foundations and other tools they manage. Yet, as gift planners know, social impact happens via gifts to organizations that carry out programs. In between, bridging between sources of charitable funds and uses of charitable funds, we have grants, outright gifts, pledges, charitable tools like charitable remainder trusts, charitable lead trusts, donor advised funds, foundations, testamentary gifts, gift annuities, and "the killer apps" that tie it all together. Advisors plan the sources. Gift planners connect to the uses.

Social capital by itself is just money on hold. Advisors can create pools of it, but need also to connect to impact via tools, programs, and projects. They can't do that without gift planners. Yet gift planners often make it hard by operating within such narrow silos with such short solicitation cycles and with no overall plan for lifetime giving that amounts to something important to donor and charity. Steven Meyers' "killer apps" and problem solving approach are much needed, and a rare bridge between these worlds of mutual unknowing. By meeting advisors half way and learning a bit of their world, you, as a gift planner, set an example and encourage advisors to follow suit and to learn a bit about your world. You might offer them this book. In return you might read one book they suggest. Out of such shared knowledge comes collaboration for the benefit of all concerned.

At this point, the advisor has gone about as far as possible without your help. What can your organization do with $5 million? Can you offer naming rights or special programs if that money comes in a big block at death? What can you offer if the money comes in at $500,000 for ten years? Or, $1 million for five years? What if the couple wants to establish a gift based on one of the "killer apps," say, a virtual endowment where the donors have a two-part pledge, first for the amount needed to maintain the program annually (the spending rate of $250,000), and then a bequest of $5 million to fully fund the endowment later; what if this corpus comes from an insurance policy or a charitable trust? What if the money comes from a foundation? From a donor-advised fund? Will you accept the $5 million in installments straight up or must all amounts be adjusted for the CPI? What if the $5 million is in the form of a strip mall? A farm? An S corporation?

Steven at the planning table with the advisors, all dedicated to the donor/ client, all in problem-solving mode, will get this gift closed. He can do that because he has lived in the Matrix, has a wary respect for it, and has the creativity and institutional support to escape it when needed. In concert with advisors, he will create a personalized umbrella gift agreement congruent with the funding pattern the donor can best afford, in the context of an overall financial plan and estate plan.

In complementing the advisory process, a process that is incomplete without it, the book you have just read is a powerful tool for the good. The time is now. Let us work together to help our best donors and clients have the impact they desire, during their lives and after they are gone, through the charities they love, and support—including yours.

**Philip Cubeta, CLU°, ChFC°, MSFS, CAP°**
The Sallie B. and William B. Wallace Chair in
Philanthropy at The American College of Financial Services

# Appendix

## Specific Counting and Reporting Guidelines

### Fundamental Principles of Campaign Counting

These principles apply specifically to organizations planning comprehensive multi-year campaigns. All of these recommendations follow from the paradigm set forth previously in this report.

1. The following **basic principles** for counting gifts should be used for the campaign:

   a. Only those gifts and pledges actually received or committed during the period of time identified for the campaign should be counted in campaign totals.

   b. The advance-gifts phase is part of the designated campaign period, and commitments reported for this phase should actually have been received or pledged during this specified period within the campaign timeframe. Defining the advance-gifts phase as part of the campaign period will also help ensure that so called "reach back" gifts are not counted. Gifts made in contemplation of a campaign (i.e., gifts for specifically defined campaign priority projects committed before the advance gift phase) must be acknowledged on all campaign reports.

   c. Gifts and pledges may be counted to only one campaign. Organizations may also wish to note maturations of commitments made to a previous campaign, but these should not be confused with new commitments secured during the campaign. The value of canceled or unfulfilled pledges should be subtracted from campaign totals when it is determined they will not be realized.

d.  If a commitment recorded in Category C (revocable commitments) in a previous campaign without a dollar figure or with only a nominal figure attached to it is realized in a current campaign, it should be recorded in Category A (outright gifts) as a current gift.

2.  **Campaign period**: All gifts and pledges to the campaign and affiliated entities acting on its behalf during the campaign period should be counted in accordance with these Guidelines. The "campaign period" refers to the total time encompassed by the active solicitation period for the campaign, including the advance-gifts phase. The normal length of a campaign is suggested to be no more than seven years. Should the campaign period exceed seven years, the expanded period should be noted on all campaign reports, news releases and marketing materials.

3.  **Pledge payment period**: The pledge payment period should not exceed five years for commitments counted in Category A, and if exceptions are approved by the Oversight Committee, the exceptions should be enumerated in campaign reports.

4.  **When to report gifts:** Outright gifts should be reported only when assets are transferred irrevocably to the institution. Deferred irrevocable gifts should be reported only when assets are transferred to the gift instrument. Revocable commitments should be reported when the gift instrument is executed and sufficient documentation is received by the charity.

5.  **Annual reporting within a multi-year campaign**: Many charities "bundle" their annual fundraising activities into a more comprehensive multi-year effort. Just as organizations now report annual results as a subset in the midst of a multi-year process (and thus keep two sets of complementary

"books"), so could charities use these guidelines to report activities in both an annual "campaign" and a multi-year "campaign."

6. **Reporting of maturations of previous commitments:** So often, development programs receive little recognition for the ultimate maturations of irrevocable and revocable deferred gifts. Development staff may not even know when these gifts have matured. This is particularly true for life income gifts—trusts, annuities and PIF funds—but sometimes also for distributions from life insurance contracts or qualified retirement plans. These matured distributions, however, have direct impact on the financial welfare of the organization. While we do not recommend that organizations count these matured distributions in campaign totals if they had been counted in a previous campaign, we do recommend that development operations report to boards and other key constituents when these distributions occur. All too often, executives and board members see the numbers when commitments are made, but lose track of the ultimate benefits when distributions take place. Closing the circle by reporting these results separately from new commitments will provide a more well-rounded picture of the impact of the entire development program on the institution and reinforce the understanding of those outside of the development office about the three dimensional and long term benefits of the work they are doing.

7. **Exclusions:** The following types of funds are excluded from campaign totals.

   a. Gifts or pledges, outright and deferred, to the extent that they have already been counted in previous campaigns, even if realized during the campaign-reporting period. (Matured commitments from previous campaign are tracked separately on the campaign reporting form).

   b. Investment earnings on gifts, even if accrued during the campaign reporting period and even if required within the terms specified by a donor (the only exception permitted to this exclusion would be interest accumulations counted in guaranteed investment instruments that mature within the timeframe of the campaign, such as zero coupon bonds).

c. Earned income, including transfer payments from medical or analogous practice plans.

d. Surplus income transfers from ticket-based operations, except for any amount equal to that permitted as a charitable deduction by the IRS/Revenue Canada.

e. Contract revenues.

f. Government funds.

1) We recognize that certain state and federal government programs requiring private matching funds bear a special relationship to the encouragement of philanthropy. Nevertheless, the difference between public and private support is profound within the American tradition. Campaigns are clearly instruments of philanthropy, while governments are usually channels for the implementation of public policy. There are instances, however, in which government-funded agencies act like private foundations in their competition and award process (e.g., NEH, NSF, FIPSE). Proposals to these agencies require attention and effort by development professionals in much the same way as do private foundations.

2) As a way of recognizing both the potential slippery slope of counting government generated funds of any kind and the legitimate development work that goes into generating grants from certain government agencies as noted above, we recommend that charitable organizations include these qualified grants as an addendum to their regular periodic report of activity (similar to matured deferred gifts) but that they not count them as part of the report of private giving. Again, the key is clarity and transparency.

8. **What to report:** All gifts, pledges and commitments falling into categories covered by these standards may be reported. However, in keeping with the spirit of these standards, it is never appropriate to set a single overall campaign goal or to report only one number when announcing campaign results. As a minimum, the following results should be available for reporting:

   a. The total of outright gifts and pledges received, reported at face value, and payable within the campaign period and post-campaign accounting period, as specified in the campaign plan.

   b. The total of irrevocable deferred commitments, which will be received at an undetermined time in the future, reported at face value.

   c. The total of revocable deferred commitments, which will be received at an undetermined time in the future, reported at estimated current value or, if the campaign goal so stipulates, reported as the number of new revocable commitments regardless of estimated value.

## Category A: Outright Gifts

1. **Definition:** Gifts that are usable or will become usable for institutional purposes during the reporting period, whether one or more years. Examples include:

   a. Cash

   b. Marketable securities

   c. Other current gifts of non-cash assets

   d. Irrevocable pledges collectible during the reporting period

   e. The gift portion of bargain sales

   f. Lead trust distributions received during the reporting period

g. Cash value of life insurance owned by the charity (net of policy loans)

h. Realized life insurance or retirement plan benefits in excess of the amounts reported in previous campaigns

i. Realized bequests in excess of the amounts reported in previous campaigns

2. **Pledges:** Pledges are counted upon receipt of the written pledge, provided the pledge is in accord with these guidelines.

a. **Pledges to make outright gifts:** Such pledges should be written and should commit to a specific dollar amount that will be paid according to a fixed time schedule. The pledge payment period, regardless of when the pledge is made, should not exceed five years. Therefore, a pledge received even on the last day of the campaign is counted in campaign totals and may be paid over a five-year period.

b. **Oral Pledges:** Oral pledges should not be reported in campaign totals. On the rare occasion when an exception is warranted, the organization should write to the individual making an oral pledge to document the commitment, place a copy of the confirmation in the donor's file and gain specific written approval from the oversight committee.

3. **Guidelines for reporting specific types of assets**

a. **Cash:** Report cash at full value as of the date received by the institution.

b. **Marketable Securities:** Marketable securities should be counted at the average of the high and low quoted selling prices on the gift date (the date the donor relinquished dominion and control of the assets in favor of the institution). If there were not any actual trades on the gift date, the fair-market value can be computed using the weighted average of the mean of the high and low trading prices on a date before and a date after the gift date, if those dates are a reasonable number of days before and after the actual gift date. If there were no actual trades in a reasonable number of days before and after the gift date, then the fair-market value is computed based on the average of the bid and the ask price on the gift date. Exactly when dominion and control has been relinquished by a donor depends on the method of delivery of the securities to the donee. These reporting standards do not address the multitude of tax rules regarding the delivery of securities by the donor to the donee.

c. **Closely held stock:**

1) Gifts of closely held stock exceeding $10,000 in value should be reported at the fair-market value placed on them by a qualified independent appraiser as required by the IRS for valuing gifts of non-publicly traded stock. Gifts of $10,000 or less may be valued at the per-share cash purchase price of the closest transaction. Normally, this transaction will be the redemption of the stock by the corporation.

2) If no redemption is consummated during the reporting period, a gift of closely held stock may be credited to campaign totals at the value determined by a qualified independent appraiser. For a gift of $10,000 or less, when no redemption has occurred during the reporting period, an independent CPA who maintains the books for a closely held corporation is deemed to be qualified to value the stock of the corporation.

d. **Gifts of property:**

1) Gifts of real and personal property that qualify for a charitable deduction should be counted at their full fair-market value. Gifts-in-kind, such as equipment and software, shall be counted at their fair-market value.

2) Caution should be exercised to ensure that only gifts that are convertible to cash or that are of actual direct value to the institution are included in value are treated like other gifts-in-kind, but so called mega gifts of software and hardware may require special care. These types of gifts can be especially complex, and institutions should exercise extreme caution in counting these gifts in campaign totals.) Gifts with fair market value exceeding $5,000 should be counted at the value placed on them by qualified independent appraiser as required by the IRS for valuing non cash charitable contributions. Gifts of $5,000 and under may be reported at the value declared by the donor or placed on them by a qualified expert.

e. **Nongovernmental grants and contracts:** Grant income from private, nongovernmental sources should be reported; contract revenue should be excluded. The difference between a private grant and contract should be judged on the basis of the intention of the awarding agency and the legal obligation incurred by an institution in accepting the award. A grant is bestowed voluntarily, without expectation of any tangible compensation. It is donative in nature. A contract carries an explicit quid pro quo relationship between the source and the institution.

f. **Realized testamentary gifts:** All bequests realized during the defined duration of the campaign should be counted at full value in campaign totals, insofar as the amount received exceeds commitments counted in a previous campaign. If a revocable testamentary commitment made during the current campaign and counted in Category C matures during the same campaign period, it should be removed from Category C and included as an outright gift in category A.

g. **Realized Retirement Plan Assets:** All gifts of retirement plan assets realized during the defined duration of the campaign should be counted at full face value in campaign totals to the extent the gift was not counted as a commitment in a previous campaign.

## Category B: Irrevocable Deferred Gifts

1. **Definition:** Gifts committed during the reporting period, but usable by the organization at some point after the end of the period. Examples include:

   a. **Split interest gifts** such as charitable gift annuities, pooled income fund shares and charitable remainder trusts in which the beneficiary designation is irrevocable.

   b. **Life estates**

   c. **Death benefit of paid up life insurance** in which the charity is both owner and beneficiary.

   d. **Irrevocable testamentary pledges or contract to make a will**

   e. **Lead trust distributions** to be made after the reporting period

2. **Charitable remainder trusts, gift annuities and pooled-income funds:** Gifts made to establish charitable remainder trusts (including charitable remainder trusts administered outside the institution) where the remainder is not subject to change or revocation, gift annuities and contributions to pooled income funds should be credited to campaign totals at face value. When additions are made to gifts that have been counted in previous campaign(s), the additions can be counted in the current campaign.

3. **Remainder interest in a residence or farm with retained life estate:** A gift of a remainder interest in a personal residence or farm should be counted at the face value.

4. **Charitable lead trusts:** Charitable lead trusts are gifts in trust that pay an income to the charity over a period of time. These payments should be counted in Category A for amounts

received during the campaign period. The remainder of the income stream to be received by the charity should be counted in Category B.

## Category C: Revocable Deferred Gifts

1. **Definition:** Gifts solicited and committed during the reporting period, but which the donor retains the right to change the commitment and/or beneficiary. Examples include:

   a. **Estate provisions**, either from a will or a living trust.

   b. **Charitable remainder trusts** in which the donor retains the right to change the beneficiary designation. When additions are made to gifts that have been counted in previous campaign(s), the additions can be counted in the current campaign.

   c. **IRAs or other retirement plan assets** in which the charitable beneficiary's interest remains revocable by the donor

   d. **Life insurance in which the donor retains ownership** (face value less any policy loans) and in which charity is owner but premiums remain due.

   e. **The portion of donor advised fund assets** due to the charity in which the charity is the owner of the DAF program.

   f. **Other revocable pledges**

2. It is difficult to put specific numbers on certain revocable commitments whose ultimate maturation value is uncertain. The numbers reported in Category C may at best be estimates and should reflect both conservative and realistic understanding of each donor's circumstances. Commitments counted nominally in category C (for example, at $1, because the charity had no information about the value) can be counted at full value in category A if they mature in a later campaign.

3. **Age minimums:**

   a. Some organizations have set a minimum age limit (often 65 or 70) for counting revocable commitments in a formal campaign. The age limit was considered necessary due to the lack of transparency in campaign counting and the fear that inclusion of revocable commitments unlikely to mature within a "reasonable" time after the end of the campaign could mislead the public about the current benefits derived from campaign activity. We recognize the importance of this issue and organizations should exercise discretion to determine if age limits are more comfortable for their circumstances.

   b. However, setting age limits is not deemed necessary in these guidelines for two reasons. First, setting initial goals that differentiate revocable deferred commitments from other immediate or irrevocable deferred gifts provides a level of transparency sufficient to eliminate the need to explain the uncertainty of timing, nature and extent of the commitment. Second, revocable deferred commitments are often only the first major commitment a donor makes to a nonprofit organization. Those who make such commitments, no matter what their age, rarely remove a charity if they are properly stewarded. And those who make such commitments often make additional commitments that are irrevocable and frequently immediate. Accordingly, campaigns should recognize all who make such commitments. These guidelines allow charitable organizations to be clear about the nature of a revocable deferred gift and differentiate such commitments from gifts that have more immediate impact on the institution.

4. **Estate provisions:** To include estate provisions in campaign totals, the following requirements must be satisfied:

   a. The commitment should specify an amount to be distributed to the organization or, if a percentage of the estate or a trust, specify a credible estimate of the value of the estate at the time the commitment is made.

b.  (Note: The decision about whether or not these types of gifts should be given campaign credit is often based on the value of the estate. At best, this requires a judgment call to be made by the campaign managers after conversation with the donor and his/her advisor.)

c.  Have verification of the commitment through one of the following forms:

  1) A letter or agreement from the donor or donor's advisor affirming the commitment.

  2) Copy of will

  3) Notification form provided by the charity, signed by donor or advisor

  4) Charitable/Deferred Pledge Agreement. A deferred pledge agreement is a legally binding document, tested in the courts of several states, that places an obligation on the estate of the issuer to transfer a certain amount to the institution. Under such agreements, the executor of the donor's estate is held legally responsible for payment of the specified amount from the estate.

d.  The campaign will carefully investigate the actual circumstances underlying the estate and be conservative in counting such commitments toward campaign totals. If any circumstances should make it unlikely that the amount pledged by bequest will actually be realized by the organization, then the commitment should be further adjusted according to specific circumstances, or not reported at all.

1.  **Retirement plan assets:**

a.  The organization may be named as the beneficiary of retirement plan assets. A testamentary pledge of retirement plan assets shall be included in campaign totals if the following requirements have been satisfied:

b. There must be a means to establish a credible estimate of the value of the retirement plan account at the time the commitment is made.

c. (Note: The decision about whether or not these types of gifts should be given campaign credit is often based on the value of the retirement plan assets at the death of the donor. At best, this requires a judgment call to be made by the campaign managers after conversation with the donor and his/her advisor.)

d. Have verification of the commitment in the form of a letter from the donor or the donor's advisor affirming the commitment.

e. The campaign will investigate carefully the actual circumstances underlying the plan and be conservative in counting such commitments toward campaign totals. If any circumstances should make it unlikely that the amount pledged will actually be realized by the organization, then the commitment should be further adjusted according to specific circumstances, or not reported at all.

## Gifts That May Be Counted in More Than One Category, Depending on the Circumstances

1. **Life insurance:** To include commitments of life insurance in campaign totals, the following requirements must be satisfied.

   a. **Ownership:**

      1) The organization should be made the owner and irrevocable beneficiary of gifts of all new policies, paid-up policies and existing policies that are not fully paid up.

      2) If the organization is the beneficiary only and not the owner of a policy, gift credit will be given but only in Category C, in the same way as credit is given to any other revocable gift commitment.

3) The remainder of these guidelines assume that the charity is the owner of the policy.

b. **Paid-up life insurance policies:** Counted at face value in Category B.

c. **Existing policies/not fully paid up:** A life insurance policy that is not fully paid up on the date of contribution, which is given to the institution during the campaign, should be counted at face value only in Category C.

d. **New policies:** Face amount of these policies should be counted in Category C.

e. **Realized death benefits.** The insurance company's settlement amount for an insurance policy whose death benefit is realized during the campaign period, whether the policy is owned by the institution or not, should be counted in campaign totals, less amounts previously counted in former campaigns.

2. **Wholly charitable trusts administered by others:**

a. A wholly charitable trust is one that is held for the irrevocable benefit of charity, where the principal is invested and the income is distributed to charitable organizations. All interests in income and principal are irrevocably dedicated to charitable purposes (as opposed to a charitable remainder or lead trust). While it is similar in that sense to an endowment fund, it is created as a freestanding entity.

b. The fair-market value of the assets, or a portion of the assets, of such a trust administered by an outside fiduciary should be counted in Category A, in the "gifts and pledges" section of campaign totals, for the year in which the trust is established, provided that the institution has an irrevocable right to all or a predetermined portion of the income of the trust. If the trustee retains or is awarded the right to designate or alter the income beneficiary, only the income should be reported and then only as it distributed.

   c. In cases where less than the entire income of the trust is to be distributed to the institution, the amount to be reported is the income to be distributed to the institution over the total income (or the stated percentage to be distributed, if the trust terms spell this out as a percentage) multiplied by the value of the trust assets. The income of the trust, thereafter, is reported as a gift.

   d. **Community and private foundations:** Gifts **to community foundations**, the income from which is irrevocably designated, in whole or in part, to the organization, and **private foundations** established solely to benefit the organization or where the organization is to receive a specified percentage of the annual income each year, are two examples of wholly charitable trusts administered by others. (Gift recognition credit will generally be given to the foundation, although the original donors or their families should certainly be kept apprised of the distributions if at all possible.)

   e. **Donor-advised funds:** Donor-advised funds are IRS-approved public charities generally managed by investment companies and community foundations that serve as conduits for gifts. The donor's contribution is made to the fund. The donor reserves the right to suggest which charities should receive the annual income. Funds will be counted like any other gift as received. If a charitable organization is entitled to receive a certain percentage of the annual distributions of a DAF, it may count the value of that percentage as if it were an irrevocable trust administered by others.

## Gifts That Change Character During a Campaign Period

   1. All campaigns, even those with twelve month duration, face the dilemma of reporting commitments that change character during the campaign period. The important point of these guidelines is that a commitment should, at the end of the campaign period, be reported only once and should reflect the final (or most recent) form of the commitment.

2. Example: It is possible for a donor to establish an irrevocable deferred gift or a revocable gift commitment that would be reported in Categories B or C, and then, for that gift to mature within the same campaign. In such cases, we recommend that the cumulative campaign report recognize the gift only in Category A, and that any previous interim report of the gift in Categories B or C be deleted. The annual report would note this change as well.

3. A donor creates a charitable remainder trust but retains the right to change the remainder beneficiary. That commitment would appear in Category C. If, later in the campaign period, the donor made the remainder beneficiary irrevocable, the commitment would shift in the cumulative campaign report to Category B and be removed from Category C. The annual report would note the shift as well.

4. Example: A charity receives a 20-year charitable lead trust paying $10,000 per year ($200,000 in total) in the first year of a five-year comprehensive campaign. The annual report in year one will note $10,000 (the amount actually received that year) in Category A and $190,000 in Category B. The cumulative comprehensive campaign report (covering all five years) will report $50,000 in Category A (the amount committed and to be received during the campaign period) and $150,000 in Category B.

   In years two through five, the annual report will again count a $10,000 cash gift with a note that this commitment had previously been reported in Category B. There would be no further reporting in the annual report for the Category B portion of the gift, since there had been no new commitment in year two.

This example is illustrated in the following chart:

### Twenty-Year Lead Trust Paying $10,000/Year

|  | Annual | Five-Year Campaign |
|---|---|---|
| **Year 1** | $10K in Cat A | $50K in Cat A |
|  | $190K in Cat B | $150K in Cat B |
| **Years 2–5** | $10K in Cat A with note | Same as before |
|  | $0 in Cat B |  |

5. Finally, we should note again that we recommend charitable organizations report the cash distributions from commitments counted in previous campaigns, but that they not count these distributions toward "new" campaign goals. We do believe, however, that completing the cycle by noting to boards and internal managers the ultimate cash benefit of deferred commitments is an important part of the development reporting process.

## Exceptions

An appropriate campaign oversight committee will have the authority to make exceptions to the foregoing for good cause on a case-by-case basis.

## Conclusion

These guidelines recommend a method for reporting gift planning activity and results more clearly and more effectively than in the past. We recognize that the real test for these or any set of guidelines will be how this reporting structure operates in practice. Therefore, we encourage charitable organizations to share with the Partnership their experiences in using these guidelines.

Source: Partnership for Philanthropic Planning, *Guidelines for Reporting and Counting Charitable Gifts*, 2nd ed. (2009). http://bit.ly/pppguidelines.

# Index

CPSIA information can be obtained at www.ICGtesting.com
Printed in the USA
LVIW01n1358280717
542650LV00002B/3